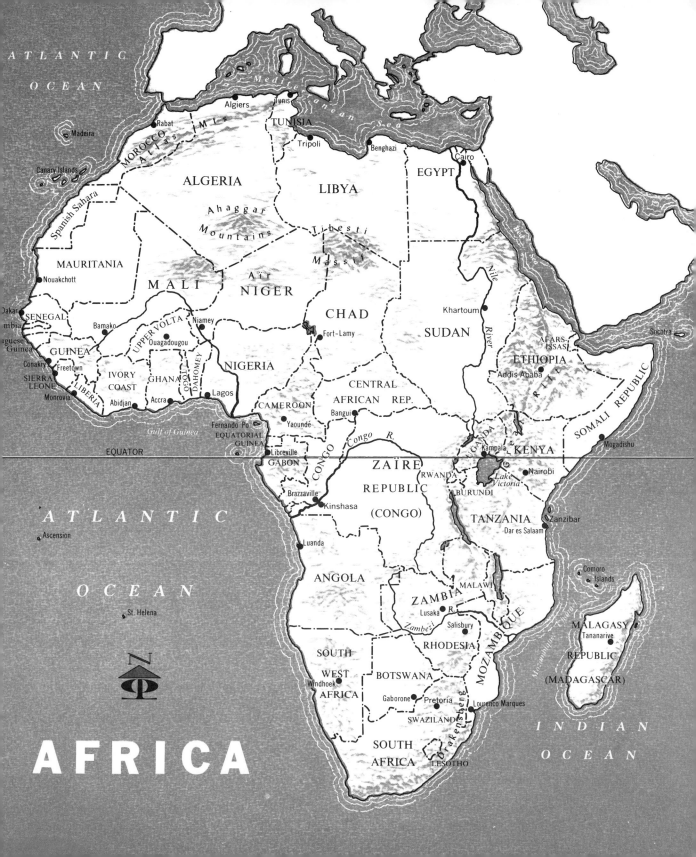

Enchantment of Africa

TUNISIA

by ALLAN CARPENTER
and BECHIR CHOUROU

Consulting Editor
Prof. Ivor G. Wilks
Department of History
Northwestern University
Evanston, Illinois

 CHILDRENS PRESS, CHICAGO

THE ENCHANTMENT OF AFRICA

Available now: Botswana, Burundi, Egypt, Kenya, Malagasy Republic (Madagascar), Rwanda, Tunisia, Uganda, Zambia
Planned for the future (six each season): Algeria, Cameroon, Central African Republic, Chad, Congo (Brazzaville), Dahomey, Equatorial Guinea, Ethiopia, Gambia, Gabon, Ghana, Guinea, Ivory Coast, Lesotho, Liberia, Libya, Malawi, Mali, Mauritania, Morocco, Niger, Nigeria, Rhodesia, Senegal, Sierra Leone, Somali Republic, South Africa, Sudan, Swaziland, Tanzania, Togo, Upper Volta, Zaïre Republic (Congo Kinshasha)

ACKNOWLEDGMENTS

Embassy of Tunisia, Washington, D.C., United States Information Service, Tunis, Tunisia; Melville J. Herskovits Library of African Studies, Northwestern University, Evanston, Illinois

Cover Photograph: Ornate Moorish doors lead to the courtyard of an old home in Sidi-Bou-Said, Allan Carpenter
Frontispiece: Village of Sfax, Photo Tap, Tunis

Series Coordinator: Michael Roberts
Project Editor: Joan Downing
Assistant Editor: Janis Fortman
Manuscript Editor: Elizabeth Rhein
Map Artist: Donald G. Bouma

LIBRARY OF CONGRESS
CATALOGING IN PUBLICATION DATA

Carpenter, John Allan, 1917-
    Tunisia.
    (Enchantment of Africa)

    SUMMARY: An introduction to the geography, people, history, government, resources, culture, and major cities of Tunisia.
    1. Tunisia—Juvenile literature.   [1. Tunisia]
I. Chourou, Bechir, joint author.   II. Title.
DT245.C36   916.1'1   73-8872
ISBN 0-516-04590-3

Contents

A True Story to Set the Scene

Twelve-year-old Ibrahim was sitting under a tree watching his few goats as they grazed. He was thinking that they were probably still hungry. There had not been much rain lately. It had rained only once or twice in the spring, and what little grass grew in the fields around Zarzia (a small coastal town in southern Tunisia) had become dry during the summer months.

That morning, Ibrahim and his parents had noticed thick, black clouds rolling in from the south, and they had hoped that these clouds would drop some rain. In the late afternoon the rain finally came. Ibrahim was so happy that he began jumping up and down. He even took off his shirt to feel the cool, refreshing water against his skin.

Ibrahim finally sat down under the tree to rest and to wait for the rain to stop. Many hours later, though, the rain was still falling—even harder than before. When it was almost dark, Ibrahim decided to return home. He gathered his goats and began the long walk.

Soon he came to a familiar little stream. That morning, there had not been even one drop of water in the stream, but now it was a furious, torrential river. When Ibrahim tried to cross it, he was thrown off balance by the gushing water and almost got carried away. He struggled back to the bank, but was horrified to see that one of his goats had been carried away.

Ibrahim was frightened. Night had fallen and he was still at least two miles

The torrential rains flooded Ibrahim's village and many others throughout the country.
PHOTO TAP. TUNIS

7

from home. It was raining harder than ever, but he knew he had to cross the river somehow. In his pocket he found a piece of rope that he had been making from palm fiber. He had intended to sell the rope, but now he used it instead. Tied around a tree, the rope became a support enabling him to cross the river. Once or twice he was almost hit by rocks and uprooted trees being carried by the rushing waters.

When he finally reached the other bank, Ibrahim began running. He had left his goats behind. The rain was blinding him. When he reached the village of Zarzia, he found that the streets were full of water, reaching to his shoulders. He swam up the main street and then started running again. After what seemed like hours, he finally reached what he thought would be his home, but nothing was there. He looked around, thinking that he might have lost his way, but there was no mistake—this was where his house used to be. Now it was gone. Ibrahim never saw his family again.

Ibrahim's tragedy was only one of thousands that took place all over Tunisia on September 25, 1969, when the country experienced the greatest catastrophe in its history. Rain fell for four days without interruption, causing major floods throughout the country. When the rain finally stopped, there were at least five hundred people dead, one hundred thousand houses destroyed, and up to fifty bridges swept away by streams that had suddenly turned into raging rivers. Hundreds of miles of roads and telephone lines, and thousands of animals, cars, and tractors were all destroyed. The southern half of the country became an immense lake. No one had ever seen such a disaster.

Nations all over the world tried to send help immediately, but airplanes could not land at the airports because the airports were covered with water. Every crop that year was totally lost. Expensive machinery in factories was heavily damaged, bringing all industrial activities to a halt. Years later, some of the damage still had not been repaired. The country's economy was set back at least five years, if not more, by this disaster.

With the help of many nations, Tunisia immediately began the long task of rebuilding. The memory of what has been described as "the flood of the millennium" will stay with every Tunisian for many years.

The Face of the Land

Located in North Africa, Tunisia is part of the geographical region that the Arabs used to call *Jazirat al-Maghreb* or "The Island of the West." Today it is known simply as the Maghreb *(Maghrib* in Arabic) to distinguish it from the Arabian Peninsula on the east. This area is not really an island, since the sea surrounds it only on the east, north, and west. Because the Sahara (which means "desert" in Arabic) is still more difficult to cross than any sea, it separates the northern part of

Africa from the rest of the continent. For all practical purposes, the Maghreb is an "island."

Tunisia makes up the eastern part of the Maghreb and is the northernmost point of Africa. It is bordered by the Mediterranean Sea on the north and east. The western border with Algeria is roughly parallel to the eastern coast as far south as the town of Nefta. Then the border starts bending eastward to meet the border with Libya at Bordj el Hattaba. This border runs in a general northeasterly direction to the coast.

The distance from the southernmost point of the country at Bordj el Hattaba to the northernmost point at Cape Blanc is about 500 miles. The average distance from east to west is about 150 miles. Tunisia is not a very large country: with a total area of about sixty-three thousand square miles, it is about the size of Michigan.

A striking characteristic of Tunisia is the sameness of its geographical features. It has no important high mountains, big rivers, or large lakes. Its highest peak, Mount Chambi, is only 5,064 feet high (compared for example with Pike's Peak in the United States, which has an elevation of 14,110 feet). Except for a few areas near the Algerian border, most of the country is practically at sea level. There are a few major rivers, but even these dry up during the hot season.

GREENERY TO DESERT

Geographers divide Tunisia into three main regions: the Tell in the north, the steppe in the center, and the Sahara in the south. The Tell is without a doubt the richest and in many ways the most important region of the country. Its southern limit is the mountains of the Great Dorsal, the eastern slopes of the Atlas Mountains that run across the entire Maghreb. As the Dorsal goes from Kasserine in the southwest (near Mount Chambi) to the peninsula of Cape Bon in the northeast, it dwindles into a series of large hills, interrupted

MAP KEY

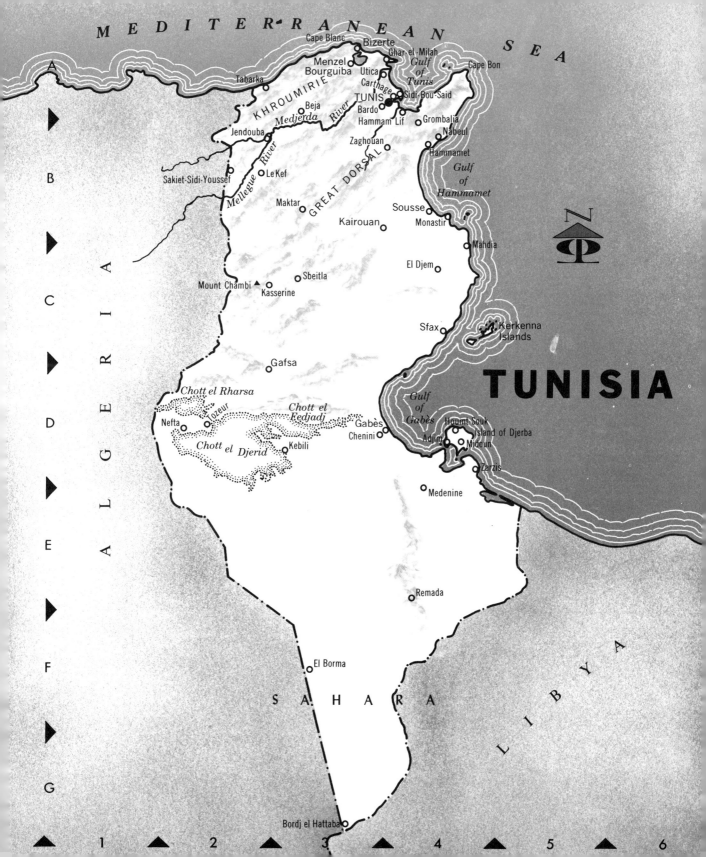

here and there by north-south corridors and valleys. Thus, the Dorsal is never a serious barrier between the northern and southern parts of the country.

It is in the Tell that the richest agricultural land is found and the country's main industries are located. It is also here that Tunis, the capital city, is located, as well as the ancient city of Carthage, today a suburb of Tunis.

Immediately to the south of the Dorsal is the central region known as the steppe. The word "steppe" is of Russian origin and refers to large, flat stretches of fairly rich land covered by grass, much like the American prairie. "Steppe," however, is not quite an appropriate name for the central region of Tunisia, which is much drier than the Russian steppe or the American prairie. From late spring to early autumn in particular, there is really very little grass to be seen.

Tunisia's steppe is, in fact, little more than a transitional zone separating the relatively rich farmland of the north from the desolate southern region of the desert

known as the Sahara. Between the cities of Maktar and Kairouan, less than seventy miles apart across the Dorsal, the change in the landscape is as dramatic as it is sudden. Green valleys and tree-covered slopes are quickly replaced by yellow, flat, and barren land. Continuing on south from Kairouan to Gafsa or Gabès, there are no abrupt changes in the landscape; it gradually becomes more barren and desertlike.

The only exception to the gradual change is a small coastal stretch in the east about seventy miles long. Called the Sahel (the Arabic word for "coast"), it includes the towns of Sousse and Mahdia. Here the influence of the sea is stronger than that of the desert and fairly rich farming is still possible. More vegetation can be seen here than in the rest of the central region.

South of an imaginary line that runs eastward from Gafsa to Gabès is the Sahara, the third major geographical region of Tunisia. Though the Sahara accounts for almost half of Tunisia's territory, less than 20 percent of the people live there. Like

Left: A village in the Tell. In the background is rich farmland typical of the area. Separating the Tell from the Sahara desert is the steppe.
Below: Men walk their donkeys along the treeless, waterless terrain of the steppe.

most other deserts, the Sahara is made up of mile after empty mile of sand and rocks. Intensely hot days are followed by intensely cold nights, with harsh winds that often provoke sandstorms.

Luxuriant, green gardens are scattered throughout the desert under a beating sun. Aldous Huxley called these gardens "little Edens"; the ancient Romans referred to them as "dark spots on the panther's coat." These are the oases, one of nature's greatest wonders. In the least expected places, water gushes plentifully from the depths of the earth to bring life to an otherwise lifeless land. The palm tree, the king of these gardens, flourishes here. Dates from these palms are the staple food of the people who live at the oases. Around each oasis many trees and plants are cultivated, such as figs, pomegranates, and various vegetables. The three most important oases in Tunisia are Tozeur, Nefta, and Chenini.

NEITHER LAKES NOR RIVERS

Because three-fourths of its territory is desert or semidesert, Tunisia has very few rivers and practically no lakes. Most of the rivers are dry, except after a rain. Since rain falls very infrequently, no bridges have been built over many of these rivers. Roads go down one bank, across the bed of the river, and up the other bank. In the middle of the riverbed and next to the road, measuring sticks are set up to indicate the depth of the water—when there is water—to help drivers determine whether or not they should try to cross.

Particularly in the steppe, the terrain is rocky, with a slight slope. When the brief but vigorous rains fall, water often accumulates quickly in large quantities. Streams become violent torrents, often causing a great deal of damage, especially to roads and telephone lines. A few hours after the rain ends the rivers are usually almost dry again.

Because there has never been much water in Tunisia's rivers, they have not cut deep, wide beds out of the earth. Fifteen or twenty feet wide at most, they would more appropriately be called streams.

In the Sahara the only water to be found is underground. This underground water is the lifeblood of the oases, and its distribution has been carefully managed for centuries. It is bought and sold, borrowed, and sometimes even fought over. Some of it springs to the surface naturally, but the rest must be pumped out.

Palm trees flourish in the oases, making the otherwise barren land of the Sahara come alive.

MINISTRY OF INFORMATION. TUNIS

In the region of the Sahara is a large depression called Chott el Djerid (the shores of Djerid). Millions of years ago, Chott el Djerid was part of a lake that linked the desert to the Mediterranean Sea. Now it is not a lake at all, but a depression filled with salty mud; it is about 170 miles long and 100 miles wide. Chott el Djerid cannot be crossed anywhere except along a carefully traced road. Anyone venturing only a few feet away from the road can find himself swallowed by the treacherous mud. In the summer, Chott el Djerid is covered by a thick layer of salt that glitters under the sun, creating many mirages. Today caravans of tourists view this awesome spectacle regularly.

Tunisia's main river, the Medjerda, is located in the northern region of the Tell. The Medjerda is the only river in Tunisia that has water in it all year. Rising in Algeria, the Medjerda flows across the entire width of Tunisia to meet the sea at a point near the town of Ghar-el-Milah. Its valley, with a total area of close to nine thousand square miles, is the most fertile land of the country.

MOUNTAINS

Like Tunisian rivers, Tunisian mountains are relatively few in number. The Dorsal is called the "backbone" of the country. Few of its peaks are more than three thousand feet high. The gentle hills of the Dorsal break up the otherwise flat land. In some parts the slopes are covered by pine trees, but generally the Dorsal has little vegetation.

Parallel to the northwestern coast is another range called the Khroumirie, with hills ranging from 1,200 to 2,400 feet high. Because the sea is so near, rains are more abundant here than in the Dorsal. Beautiful forests of cork trees nourished by these rains give this area a permanently green appearance unmatched anywhere else in the country.

CLIMATE

Although geographers label Tunisia's climate as Mediterranean in the north and Saharan in the south, tourists vacationing there think of it simply as beautiful. Temperatures rarely go below forty degrees Fahrenheit, and the sun shines in a cloudless sky for an average of ten hours every day—fourteen hours during June and July and seven hours during December and January. (England, in comparison, has an average of four hours of sun each day and France has five hours.)

The great amounts of sunshine in Tunisia are matched by little rainfall. Snowfall is practically nonexistent. Most of the rain falls between December and February. Rainfall reaches up to sixty inches a year in the Khroumirie but only six inches a year in Gafsa, on the edge of the desert. Temperatures in the north are often as high as in the desert, and droughts are frequent throughout the country.

Four Children of Tunisia

QARIM OF TABARKA

In the summertime Qarim wakes up very early in the morning, dashes through the back yard, and splashes in the sea. He swims for a while, comes home for breakfast, puts on his hiking boots, and crosses Tabarka's main street toward the mountains, where he hikes with his friends. No other town in Tunisia has both beaches and mountains. Tabarka's beaches are on the Mediterranean coast, about ten miles away from the Algerian border, and its mountains are the Khroumirie.

Qarim attends the local primary school. His favorite subject is history and he is especially interested in the history of Tabarka. Tabarka was founded about 2,800 years ago by Phoenician traders and was known as *Thabraca*, which meant "bushy and shaded place." Under the

Romans, it had a busy harbor from which ships sailed to Rome, loaded with wheat, marble, wood, leather, and wool. Since that time, it has been occupied at various times by pirates, Christian missionaries,

Italians, Turks, and finally French. After the French occupied it and the rest of Tunisia in 1881, many Frenchmen came to settle near Tabarka. They liked this area because the landscape is very similar to that of France.

Throughout its long history, Tabarka was a tiny, quiet village whose main activity was the shipping of cork that was harvested in the surrounding mountains. Qarim thinks that is quite surprising, for today Tabarka is a thriving, growing community. Several small factories were built to process the cork and a new port is being built. When the port is completed, the processed cork can be shipped directly to Europe. Qarim hopes he will have the opportunity to ride on one of these ships. All his life he has seen the Mediterranean Sea, but never has he been across it.

Qarim did not have to go to school to learn about the great number of tourists who have been coming to Tabarka in the recent years, for his father talks about them every day. Qarim's father owns one of Tabarka's finest restaurants. It specializes in shrimp and lobster caught in the Mediterranean. Many people come all the way from the capital city of Tunis to have dinner there.

The busiest week of the year at the restaurant is during the coral festival in June. Tabarka is famous for the coral found in its offshore reefs. The coral festival attracts thousands of Tunisian and foreign visitors. This is Qarim's favorite time of the year. During the week-long festival many activities are organized, such as skin diving for coral, folk dances, and picnics.

Sometimes in winter, Qarim's father leaves the restaurant in the hands of an assistant. Then he acts as a guide for groups of hunters. Occasionally Qarim is allowed to go along on the hunts for wild boars, which are very dangerous animals.

In a year or so, Qarim will graduate from the primary school and will then have to leave Tabarka and his parents, brothers, and sisters. He will attend high school in Jendouba, thirty miles away, and will come home on weekends. Maybe he will be able to convince his father that since he is old enough to go away to school, he is old enough to go boar hunting more often.

Qarim would like to go to the merchant marine school after high school to learn to become a ship captain. As the oldest son in the family, however, he knows that his father will probably want him to take over the restaurant.

HABIBA OF MONASTIR

After almost a month of preparations, Habiba's home city was finally ready for

Qarim likes to watch the fishing boats and imagine they are Phoenician trading ships.

ABDELHAMID KAHIA, A.I.D.

19

what had been a long-awaited occasion. Thousands of people were lining the main avenue and Habiba—along with her mother, three sisters, and two brothers—was right in the front row. The occasion was President Bourguiba's birthday, and the whole town had come out to greet its most illustrious son. After what seemed like a very long time, a policeman riding a beautiful, white motorcycle with red, flashing lights and a loud siren sped by. The presidential car could not be far behind! The crowd began to cheer and to shout, "Long live Bourguiba!" Before she realized what was happening, Habiba found herself right next to a red jeep crowded with people, including the president and his wife Wassila, who were smiling and waving. Though Habiba was excited, she was also a bit frightened, for she was being pushed and shoved by all the people who were trying to shake the president's hand. At least she had been able to glimpse the president and his wife. After some struggle, Habiba finally got away from the wild crowd and began to look for her brothers and sisters.

Walking back home with her family, her feet hurting and part of her dress torn, Habiba tried once again to imagine how Monastir used to be. Her father likes to tell his children that before Tunisia became independent in 1956, Monastir was just a little village. Though most of the people who lived there were farmers with only small incomes from olive trees or fishing, they sent their children to school to give them a chance for a brighter future. That is why so many of Tunisia's leaders are from Monastir.

After independence President Bourguiba had the whole town rebuilt. Today Monastir has large avenues lined with trees, beautiful parks with flowers and fountains, modern buildings, and even an international airport. Many houses were also built and the townspeople rent them for very reasonable prices. Habiba and her family live in one of these houses. It has five big rooms, electricity, running water, and a yard in which Habiba's mother grows vegetables. Though the family does not yet have a refrigerator or a stove, they do have a television set and a transistor radio. Habiba likes her house because it is clean and cheerful.

After the parade Habiba and her father stopped at the mosque (a place of worship for the people of the Moslem faith) where her father works. He is proud to be the caretaker of Monastir's newest and prettiest mosque. Habiba loves the main prayer room, with its gleaming, white marble columns, elegant chandeliers, and thick, white carpets. There were only a few people inside the mosque because it was not a Friday. On Friday afternoons, the mosque is jammed with people who come for communal prayer.

On the way home Habiba and her father passed Habiba's school, a modern building with large, sunny classrooms. Some of the teachers are from France and the United States. After Habiba graduates, she would like to attend the university in Tunis, but her father says that she will be old enough

Habiba and her family attended the parade in Monastir for Habib Bourguiba's birthday.

to marry and raise a family by then. Habiba hopes that by the time she graduates, her father will change his mind. If he does, Habiba wants to study hotel management and work in one of the new hotels in Monastir. Since the hotels were built, many tourists have visited Monastir. Tourism is rapidly becoming more important in the area than farming. All of this has happened because President Bourguiba took an earnest interest in his home town, and the people of Monastir are grateful to him.

MBAREK OF KASSERINE

Mbarek woke up slowly and looked around him. He saw four light pink walls with a few pictures pinned on them, a table in a corner with books on it, a chair, and a window through which a ray of sun was coming. He saw the same things he had seen every day for the last two years and once again, he began to cry.

Mbarek is a Bedouin. For as long as he could remember and up until the day when he came to Kasserine, he and eighteen members of his family— parents, brothers and sisters, uncles and aunts, and cousins— had roamed the country. With their camels, sheep, and goats, they went wherever there were crops to be harvested and wherever there was good grazing land for the animals. From wheat fields in the north to the palm trees of the oases in the south and from citrus and olive groves along the coast to the baobab trees in the

west, theirs was a life of perpetual travel. When one job was done, they moved on to the next one. When the sun set, they set up their tents for the night—no matter where they were.

What a wonderful life that was, thought Mbarek as he was sitting in his bed. In the few years of his life, he had come to know every hill, every beach, every stream, and every dune in his country. He had learned to care for animals, to harvest fruit, and to understand nature.

Mbarek's family had often discussed how life had become increasingly difficult for the Bedouins lately. More and more farmers had begun using strange-looking machines to plant and harvest their crops, and the Bedouins were having difficulty finding work. They were also frequently stopped by the police along the highways and told to go back to their original villages or to their ancestors' land and stay there. Mbarek's father had heard radio speeches by President Bourguiba promising help to the Bedouins if they would build homes and find steady work. But how, Mbarek wondered, can people know that a true Bedouin could never settle in one place forever and that his life would be miserable if he were forced to do so?

Younger Bedouins are beginning to face the harsh fact that someday soon their nomadic way of life will no longer enable them to earn a living. As a result, many have gone to cities and towns to work in such places as factories, mines, and garages, as did Mbarek's brother Jilani four years earlier. He came to Kasserine,

Mbarek's family, like all Bedouins, travels from place to place in a caravan.

where the government had just finished building a big paper manufacturing factory. Jilani was hired there as a janitor. At night he attends adult classes to learn how to read and write. In a year or two, he hopes to become a machine operator, which will pay more money.

Jilani had trouble getting a job when he first came to Kasserine. No one had wanted to hire someone who could not read or write. Because Jilani did not want the same thing to happen to his younger brother, he convinced his father to let Mbarek live with him in Kasserine so Mbarek could attend school. Mbarek did not like that idea at all, but he had to obey his father and older brother's wishes. He would never tell his brother, but he has been miserable in Kasserine, particularly the first year he was there. At school he

was the oldest first-grader in the class. Many of the children wore nice clothes and shoes because their parents were engineers at the factory. They made fun of Mbarek's clothes and accent. This made his first year at school very difficult. Fortunately, his teacher always tried to help him in every way possible.

Mbarek is slowly getting used to his new life. Every once in awhile, he climbs Mount Chambi. Sometimes he runs into a caravan of Bedouins and has long talks with them. Mbarek also likes to go to the train station. There he watches workers unload alfalfa that is harvested in the desert and load big rolls of paper that will be taken to Tunis and other cities.

In the evening, he and his brother help each other with their homework while Mabrouka, Jilani's wife, fixes tea. The

23

best time, though, is when their parents, brothers, and sisters come to Kasserine to spend the winter with them. Mbarek wants to finish school as soon as possible and get a good job. Then he and his brother will be able to get a bigger house and maybe even convince their father to bring the rest of the family to live there permanently.

AYAD OF MIDOUN

Ayad lives in Midoun, a small village in the northeastern part of the island of Djerba. Lying about 350 miles south of Tunis and only a few miles off the mainland, the island of Djerba has been described in history and literature for many centuries. Legend says that Djerba is the place that Homer (a famous Greek epic poet) describes in *The Odyssey,* where Ulysses was held captive by the enchantress Calypso.

It is known that the Romans built a town there called Meninx. There are many remains of this town, including the causeway that links the island to the mainland. Truly an engineering masterpiece, this road across the sea is four miles long and thirty-three feet wide. It is still used today—about twenty-two hundred years after it was built.

The town of Midoun, where Ayad lives, is typical of the many villages that are scattered around the island. In the middle of the village a large plaza is surrounded by small shops owned by such tradesmen as a barber, a butcher, and a blacksmith. There are also a post office, two primary schools (one for boys and one for girls), a

There are many Roman ruins near Ayad's village on the island of Djerba.

few cafés, and a mosque. There are no houses in the town; people live all around the village on farms called *menzels.*

Many different peoples live on the menzels. Some of them, like Ayad's family, are descendants of blacks who escaped from slave caravans and came to the island of Djerba. Others are Jews, whose ancestors first came to the island as long ago as 550 B.C., after the destruction of the temple described in the Old Testament.

The menzel on which Ayad lives is about two miles from the town. It has about four acres of land with many palm trees and a few apricot, almond, and fig trees. In one corner of the menzel is the *housh,* where the family lives. The housh is a fortresslike structure that is square in shape. In the center is a courtyard, which usually has a tree planted in the middle; the courtyard is flanked by a large room on each side. Since practically no menzel on the island has running water, each has a *majen,* a large, cisternlike water tank dug in the ground in which rainwater is collected for drinking. Menzels also have wells with water which is used mostly for washing and irrigation. This water is a bit too salty for drinking.

On his way to town one day, Ayad began thinking of his father. It had been over a year since he had seen him. Thousands of other children in Djerba had not seen their fathers in a long time, either. Because the island has almost no natural resources and water is scarce, farms cannot produce a surplus to sell and many of the Djeraba (the inhabitants of the island) have had to go to the mainland to earn a living. Traditionally, they have gone to Tunis to operate grocery stores. So many of them have done this that the word "Jerbi" (another name for a native of Djerba) has come to mean "grocer."

Ayad's father was no exception. At the age of fifteen, he left for Tunis to work as an apprentice in a grocery store. He has returned to Djerba only for brief visits. After a few years, he had saved enough money to open his own store in Tunis. Three years ago, he decided to go to France and open a store in Paris, where he could earn more money. He left, and that is where he has been ever since, except for one visit home. Every month he sends money to his family in Midoun.

Ayad's father hopes to return home in a few years and turn his store over to his younger son. Usually the eldest son inherits the family business but Ayad's older brother, after much arguing and cajoling, was allowed to go to a university. Today he is an anthropologist studying ancient customs on Djerba.

Ayad wants to go to Paris, but not to be a grocer. Ayad's ambition is to go to a university in France, as his brother did. He wants to be an architect. The tourist industry is growing rapidly on Djerba and many new buildings will be needed. Even now, many Djeraba are giving up the grocery business and coming back to the island to help develop the tourist industry there. After studying architecture, Ayad wants to return to Djerba to participate in the booming building business.

Tunisia Yesterday

Millions of years ago, North Africa was a jungle similar to the one found today in Equatorial Africa and in parts of Central and South America. It was hot and humid, and the thick rain forest was populated with wild animals such as elephants, rhinoceroses, hippopotamuses, zebras, and giraffes. People also lived there, but little is known about the earliest of them except that they lived on plants, roots, raw fish, and shellfish. Slowly these people learned to make crude tools out of stone. They used them to cut branches for animal traps. Some of these tools have been uncovered in recent years by archaeologists, who believe that the tools are about two million years old. Not much else, however, is known about these early—and perhaps original—inhabitants of North Africa. No other traces of their existence have yet been found.

During this time, the climate of the region was changing: it was becoming much drier. New plant and animal life that could adapt to this change was developing. Trees such as cork began to grow there, and animals such as the hippopotamus migrated to the south.

Two groups of people then appeared. The first, known as the Maurusiens, came about 12,000 B.C. and settled along the northern coast of Africa. The second group, called Capsiens, appeared about 7000 B.C. and settled near present-day Gabès in southern Tunisia. The Capsiens eventually spread north and chased the

A dolmen near Naktar. A dolmen is a prehistoric monument consisting of two or more upright stones that support a horizontal stone slab.

27

Maurusiens either into the mountains or out of Africa. These groups left remains that show evidence of a relatively advanced civilization.

The Capsiens lived in villages and had permanent houses. They used sophisticated tools to hunt and kill animals for food, and they cooked their food rather than eating it raw. From the cave drawings that have been discovered, it appears that these people were some of the earliest artists. Unfortunately, little is known about their daily lives or their religion.

From about 5000 B.C. on, many different peoples invaded North Africa, bringing with them bronze tools and new farming methods. At some time during that period, there also appeared a nomadic group called Lybiens, who immigrated from the east. There is evidence that the Lybiens are the ancestors of the North African Berbers, a group that still lives in the mountains of North Africa.

Until about 1200 B.C. the Lybiens led a nomadic life. They were grouped in clans, each clan headed by a chief. The clans were formed into loose federations but often fought among themselves. The Lybiens worshiped the sun and the moon, as well as animals such as the ram, believing that these animals represented awesome and obscure supernatural spirits. They also worshiped the dead, who they buried in sitting positions after they reduced the bodies to skeletons and painted the bones red. Because the Lybiens also put jewelry and containers for food and drink in the graves, they probably believed in some

kind of life after death. All graves faced east and were covered by large stones and mounds of earth.

PHOENICIA

About 1900 B.C. Phoenicia was a rich and powerful nation. From its capital of Tyre (located in modern Lebanon), its famous sailors went to the far reaches of the Mediterranean and established trading posts in what are now Sardinia, Sicily, Spain, and North Africa. In Tunisia they founded Utica (near present-day Tunis), Hippo Zarytus (Bizerte), and Hadrumete (Sousse).

The Phoenicians traded such goods as wood products and textiles, as well as wool, silk, and perfumes which they had imported from India and Arabia. They traded these products in Spain and Morocco for gold, silver, and bronze. Without maps or compasses, Phoenician sailors were able to navigate with the help of what they called the Phoenician star (the North Star), which always seems to have the same position in the sky. Their trips were long and dangerous. To minimize the danger, the Phoenicians traveled only by day and not too far from the coastline.

The Spaniards and Moroccans did not let the Phoenician sailors come ashore because they were afraid that the sailors would find the mines. Therefore, when the sailors reached a trading post, they put their merchandise on the beach, lit a big fire to signal their presence, and went back to their ships. People then came, examined the merchandise, left the amount of gold and other metals they thought covered the value of the goods, and went away without taking these goods. The ship captain then went on shore and examined the metals. If the amount was not satisfactory, he left it there and went back to his ship to wait for the people to bring more. When the proper amount was obtained, it was taken aboard, the fire was put out, and the ships went back to sea. The Greek historian Herodotus, who reported this unique practice (today called *dumb barter*) pointed out that "neither party was dishonest."

CARTHAGE

In 815 B.C. the king of Tyre died and left power to his son Pygmalion and his daughter Elissa, also known as Dido. Pygmalion, however, excluded his sister from the throne. When he assassinated her husband Acerba, Elissa felt her own life threatened and fled from Tyre. In 814 B.C. she and à few companions landed near Utica. She asked King Hiarbas, who ruled the area, for a piece of land where she could settle. The king agreed to give her as much land as could be outlined by the hide of a bull. The shrewd Elissa took the largest hide she could find and cut it in small pieces to form a rope long enough to encircle a hill. On top of that hill, a small village was built, which Elissa called Quart Hadasht, or "new city." Later the town became known as Carthage. Thus, the first major foreign occupation of Tunisia had begun.

Little by little the town grew and prospered. The Carthaginians traded in the Mediterranean and soon controlled most of the trading posts of the western Mediterranean. With their wealth they built beautiful homes, some of which reached as high as six stories. They also built strong fortifications around the city and built two large harbors, one for merchant ships and one for warships. The Carthaginians then began moving inland, easily conquering most of the territory that makes up modern Tunisia and the eastern part of Algeria. The Berbers who lived there had to pay taxes to the Carthaginians in the form of land, labor, and service in the army or navy. Elsewhere in North Africa, the Carthaginians established small colonies beyond the coast, which the Phoenicians had never done. They also made treaties of good will and friendship with the local Berber rulers. The empire they established was known as the Punic Empire.

Many Berbers who had contact with the Carthaginians began to settle in towns and acquire new farming skills. They learned how to grow fruits such as figs, pomegranates, olives, and grapes, all of which the Carthaginians had introduced to North Africa. Carthage did not need to buy food from abroad and was able to export food in large quantities. Thus, Carthage prospered and soon ruled the Mediterranean.

The Berbers soon learned farming skills from the Carthaginians. Here men climb trees to harvest dates.

In the sixth century B.C., Greece occupied southern Italy, part of Sicily, and Marseilles (in present-day France). It was attempting to expand in the Mediterranean and was threatening the Punic Empire in Corsica, Sardinia, and eastern Sicily. Not willing to accept any challenge to its supremacy, Carthage declared war on Greece, conquering Marseilles and

Corsica in 535 B.C. and Sicily a few years later. For nearly four hundred years, Carthage was the uncontested master of the Mediterranean.

THE DECLINE OF CARTHAGE

Many severe weaknesses lay hidden beneath the apparent might of the Punic Empire. The Carthaginians had spread themselves too thin. Most of their colonies were far away from the capital and could not be effectively controlled. Also, the Carthaginians relied too heavily on mercenaries (hired soldiers) for their defense and the defense of their colonies. The mercenaries proved to be unreliable at times of hardship. Because of these two problems, the frequent uprisings in the colonies were suppressed only with a great deal of difficulty.

Close to the capital itself, the empire had to face still another problem. Many Berber groups, whom the Carthaginians had encouraged to become farmers, had grown rich and powerful over the years. They began to challenge their rulers, first by not paying taxes, then by waging armed revolts against them. They even sided with foreign invaders against Carthage.

All of these problems crystallized in 264 B.C. when the first of three wars between Carthage and Rome—known as the Punic Wars—took place. Until then Rome had been neither a threat nor a challenge to Carthage. In fact, the two even had a common enemy: Greece. After Rome finally occupied all of Italy, it decided to move into Sicily. Since Carthage then occupied Sicily, Rome's move directly conflicted with Carthage's interests.

The first Punic War lasted for twenty-three years and ended with victory for Rome. It not only cost Carthage many of its overseas colonies, but more importantly it showed that Carthage no longer had supremacy of the Mediterranean. Furthermore, the war triggered widespread revolts among the Berbers and mutinies in the army. Taking advantage of that situation, Rome moved in and took away Carthage's remaining overseas territories.

Carthage, however, did not give up. Hamilcar, a famous Punic general, set out to conquer Spain, where enough gold was collected to raise a new army. In 219 B.C. a Punic army, riding elephants and headed by Hamilcar's son Hannibal, invaded Italy from the northwest and won great victories. When Hannibal finally arrived near Rome, however, he did not have enough forces left to attack it. This factor gave Rome enough time to organize a counterattack, and Hannibal was driven to southern Italy. Spain—Hannibal's source of supplies—was retaken, and Carthage, attacked and defeated, became a Roman protectorate. Thus ended the Second Punic War in 201 B.C. It cost Carthage its navy, army, elephants, and part of its African empire. This war also saw the rise of the Berbers as a new force in North Africa. They had become so strong that the side on which they fought was almost sure to win. They could have prevented the Romans from landing in Carthage, but chose instead to fight with them against the Carthaginians.

THE DESTRUCTION OF CARTHAGE

By the beginning of the second century B.C., the Punic Empire controlled only Carthage and a small territory around it. The Berbers controlled the rich plains of Constantine (in present-day Algeria). The Berber king, Massinissa, had gained the allegiance of many Berber clans and planned to unify all of North Africa under his control. Carthage had signed a treaty with Rome giving it the right to maintain an army or to wage wars. Since Massinissa had helped the Romans in North Africa, it was easy for him to begin occupying Punic territories west of Carthage.

At first Rome did not intervene against the Berbers. When Carthage was threatened, however, Rome understood the ambitions of the Berbers. Because the Romans did not want a new power to rise in North Africa, they attacked Carthage, burned it to the ground, and covered it with salt—rather than allow it to fall into Berber hands. This move is known as the Third Punic War (149-146 B.C.). During this war the Carthaginians heroically defended their town, street by street and house by house, but were systematically massacred by the Romans. The site of the city and all of the coastal region of modern

Tunisia were made a Roman province and given the name of *Africa*. Thus ended the Punic era and the first foreign occupation of Tunisia; it had lasted for 654 years and would be followed by 576 years of Roman rule.

THE ROMAN PROTECTORATE

Having conquered all of North Africa, the Romans decided to rule it indirectly through Berber kings named as governors. King Massinissa, the main Berber governor, died in 148 B.C. and his son Micipsa inherited a rich territory that covered most of present-day Algeria. Micipsa's nephew, Jugurtha, was a brilliant and courageous army officer who wanted to get rid of Roman control. Jugurtha eventually inherited one-third of his uncle's kingdom. The other two-thirds went to Micipsa's sons, Hiempsal and Adherbal, who resented having to share the power with their cousin Jugurtha. They refused to support Jugurtha's efforts to get rid of Roman control. Jugurtha had Hiempsal killed and waged war against Adherbal, who fled to Rome to ask for help. Adherbal, too, was eventually killed and Jugurtha became the master of North Africa.

In 112 B.C. Rome finally realized the threat that Jugurtha presented and decided to eliminate him. War was proclaimed, but what the Romans thought would be a short campaign turned out to be a long and costly one. After six years Jugurtha was still not beaten. He was finally defeated in 106 B.C. by the Roman general Marius and thrown into a dungeon in Rome, where he died two years later.

From then on the Romans continued to put down occasional uprisings by Berber kings. It was not until 46 B.C., however, that the Romans decided to rule North Africa directly. The area was then officially divided into four provinces: Africa, Numidia, Eastern Mauritania, and Western Mauritania. These areas roughly corresponded to what is now Tunisia, eastern and western Algeria, and Morocco, respectively. Each was governed by Roman officials.

Of all these provinces, Rome considered Africa to be the most important. It was administered by a proconsul (governor) who was nominated by the Senate in Rome and was responsible to the Senate rather than to the Roman emperor. The rulers of the other provinces were of much lower rank. Africa was already very rich agriculturally and it was developed even further to become the "granary of Rome." Carthage was rebuilt in 44 B.C. and it became the capital of Africa; other towns were developed and new ones founded. An excellent road network and a fine irrigation system were established. This system's most striking feature was the aqueduct that carried water from Zaghouan to Carthage, a distance of more than twenty-five miles.

For more than three hundred years, Africa was blessed by peace. The riches of Carthage were famous throughout the Roman Empire, even rivaling those of the

This aqueduct carried water from Carthage to Zaghouan, more than twenty-five miles.

city of Rome. Historians report that Roman rule was lenient and beneficial to the Berbers.

There were still a large number of Berbers, however, who as slaves had to work for the rich estate-owners or to serve in the army. When Christianity came to Africa around A.D. 180, these Berbers embraced it, for they thought it would bring them salvation from their condition.

In 238, the powerful Roman proconsul Gordien declared Africa's independence from Rome. This declaration started a series of wars in Africa not only between Rome and Carthage, but among Carthaginian leaders who claimed the seat of power. Taking advantage of this unstable situation, the Berbers attacked the Romans throughout North Africa. From then on, it was only a matter of time before the Romans lost their power in North Africa and throughout their empire.

In 395 the Roman Empire was divided into two parts, Eastern and Western. This division critically weakened the empire, and when a new group of invaders appeared in Africa, no one was in a position to resist them.

33

*Architecture is all that is left in Tunisia to show that Romans once ruled the country.
Left: Ruins of buildings at El Djem. Above: Ruins of Roman baths at Carthage.*

VANDALS AND BYZANTINES

The Vandals were originally from Scandinavia. They had first invaded eastern Europe and then moved westward, conquering part of France and settling in Spain. Their chief, Genseric, landed in Western Mauritania in 429, and in a series of lightning-quick campaigns he subdued all of North Africa. In 439 he entered Carthage and made it the capital of the Vandals. From there, Genseric set out to conquer Sicily, Corsica, and Sardinia. In 455 he entered Rome itself.

Vandal rule did not last after Genseric's death in 477. A struggle for succession to the throne followed, which weakened the Vandals considerably. When the emperor of Byzantium attempted to retake Carthage in 534, he found little resistance. Dominance by the Vandals, which lasted a little less than a century and left practically no trace of any kind, had ended, leaving North Africa to the Byzantines.

The Byzantines, however, proved to be as unstable as their predecessors, the Vandals. During the 113 years of Byzantium's existence (534-647), it never attempted to control all of North Africa, limiting itself instead to what is now Tunisia and part of Algeria. The Berbers who lived outside of these territories continuously attacked the Byzantines. They were soon joined by people living in Tunisia who revolted against their harsh and, at the time, inhuman rulers. When yet another group of in-

A mosque in a village. The Arabs brought the Islamic religion to Tunisia.

vaders—the Arabs—appeared in 647, the Byzantines were able to offer little resistance.

Until the arrival of the Arabs, none of the foreign peoples who occupied Tunisia tried to integrate the local Berbers into their society. There was some inter-marriage between the various groups, and some Berbers chose to adopt the way of life of the foreigners. In general, though, the foreign rulers ignored the local people as long as the people worked for them and did not threaten their position as rulers. This fact made the Berbers resent the alien rulers and attempt, whenever possible, to eliminate them. Furthermore, even though some of the early foreigners spent many centuries in Tunisia, they never brought their religion, culture, or customs to Tunisia in any significant way. Today the only trace of their presence is in the form of buildings. This was not to be the case of the Arabs.

THE COMING OF ISLAM

The Arabs first came to Tunisia in 647. They stayed only a short while, probably just long enough to learn whether Tunisia was worth conquering, and returned home immediately after defeating the Byzantines at Sbeitla in southern Tunisia. The Arabs returned twenty-three years later, this time with the intention of conquest. Their leader Ugba-Ibn-Nafi founded the city of Kairouan in 670. The city became the starting point for future Arab expansions and later grew into a great metropolis. Its mosque, which still exists, was a religious and intellectual center famous throughout the Moslem world.

Unlike previous invaders, the Arabs were not interested simply in acquiring an empire, but more importantly sought to introduce the Islam religion and the Arabic language. The Arabs realized, however, that these two goals could not be achieved until they established themselves as rulers. Consequently, they waged a series of wars against the Berbers and the Byzantines. Defeating the Byzantines, the Arabs took Carthage in 695. A large group of Berbers, led by a Berber princess called Kahina, were defeated in 702. Kahina's followers became the first Berbers to embrace Islam. With their help, the Arabs went on to conquer all of North Africa and most of Spain, and had an amazing success in establishing their religion everywhere they went. The spread of the Arabic language, however, was much slower. In some isolated areas it was not adopted by the people until modern times.

THE MOSLEM BERBERS GAIN POWER

Though Islam quickly took root in Tunisia, Arab rule did not. Between 670 and 973, *Ifriqya* (as Tunisia was then called by the Arabs) was ruled by governors appointed at Baghdad, the capital of Iraq and of the Arab world. After 800, power in Ifriqya was concentrated within a few families and was even passed down from father to son in dynasties, but these dynasties still ruled in the name of Baghdad. The two most famous dynasties of the period were the Aghlabids, the descendants of Ibrahim ben Aghlab, and the Fatimids, the descendants of the prophet Mohammed. The Fatimids moved from Kairouan, the capital of Ifriqya, to a new city founded in 916 called Mahdia (located on the eastern coast).

By this time, ties with Baghdad were almost completely broken. Fatimid rule was particularly harsh on the local population and it led to bloody but unsuccessful revolts. In 973 the Fatimids conquered Egypt and founded the city of Cairo, which became their capital.

Al-Mu'izz, who was then the head of the Fatimid dynasty, left the government of Ifriqya in the hands of Bologuin, a member of the Ziri family. Bologuin remained faithful to his masters in Cairo all his life, but his descendants, who remained in power for nearly seventy-five years, slowly broke away from Egypt. In 1050 they switched their allegiance back to Baghdad, establishing a dynasty of their own.

The Fatimids were enraged by this act of repudiation, but they had little money and no army. In 1051 they sent the Banu Hilal and the Banu Silaim, Arab nomadic groups, to invade Kairouan. Ibn Khaldun, the great Tunisian historian of the fourteenth century, wrote: "The Arabs entered the city and began their work of devastation, looting stores, destroying public buildings, and sacking houses. Everything in the city was taken away or destroyed. Thus this great catastrophe was consumed."

The Arabs moved north, allowing their animals to destroy farms and fields. This invasion had another, and perhaps more profound, influence on Ifriqya. Unlike the original Arab invaders of the seventh century, these Arabs brought their families and soon intermarried with the Berber nomads, thereby spreading the Arabic language and culture.

For a century Ifriqya was in total chaos. The Zirid dynasty crumbled and no dynasty took its place. Ifriqya was split under the rule of numerous, small Berber clans. During this time, the country came under attack first from the Roman Catholic pope in Rome (1087), then from the Normans who captured Mahdia in 1148.

In 1159 a powerful Islamic Berber dynasty from Morocco, the Almohades, decided to wage a *jihad,* or holy war, against the non-Moslems (called *infidels* by the Moslems). When victory was achieved, the Almohades appointed one of their members, Abu Hafs, governor of Ifriqya; then they returned to Morocco. Geographical distance encouraged the governor to acquire more and more power on his own. Finally, in 1230 Zakariya (who had succeeded his father as governor) broke away from the Almohades and created the Hafsite dynasty, which ruled Ifriqya for three and one-half centuries. It was undoubtedly the greatest dynasty in Tunisian history.

THE HAFSITE DYNASTY

In 1236 Zakariya made Tunis, which was then just a small town, the capital city. It was during this period that the medina, which is today the old section of the city of Tunis, was built. The Hafsids (members of the Hafsite dynasty) were attacked by European Christians, including the Crusaders led by Louis IX of France (who died in Carthage in 1270) and Alphonse V of Aragon (Spain) in 1432. Moslems from Libya attacked in the fourteenth century. The Hafsids, however, were able to withstand most of these attacks easily.

Music, art, architecture, and poetry began to flourish in Tunis under the Hafsids. It was during this period that Ibn Khaldun lived—the great historian known as the "father of modern sociology."

Many Moslems from Spain and Jews from all over the Mediterranean fled to Tunis because they were being persecuted. The Jews in particular, along with some Christians, developed trade with Europe. For the first time in Tunisian history, foreign ambassadors came to live in Tunis. By the end of the fifteenth century, life had been so peaceful and easy in Tunis for so long that the country became dangerously self-satisfied. No advances in science or technology were made. The Hafsids made little attempt to adopt firearms which were in wide use elsewhere. Since they were unable to defend themselves, the Hafsids could not prevent Turkish pirates from using the town of Tunis as a refuge.

THE SPANISH PROTECTORATE

Two new powers, Spain and Turkey, were becoming important in the early 1500s. For forty years these two powers fought for control of North Africa. In 1534, after having occupied the city of Algiers, the Ottoman Empire of the Turks conquered Bizerte, Tunis, and even Kairouan. Unable to stop the Turks, the sultan (king) of Tunis asked the king of Spain, Carlos V, for his aid. Sensing that Turkey might seek to replace the Arabs in Spain after Carlos V had just ousted them from his territory, he decided to help the sultan.

Carlos V retook Tunis in 1535 and Monastir in 1540, establishing a Spanish protectorate over Tunis. The protectorate, however, was destined to be short-lived. In 1574, after what is reported to have been an awesome battle, Tunis fell at the hands of the Ottoman Empire.

TURKISH TUNISIA

Though Turkish rule in Tunisia legally did not end until independence, very little change occurred in the country during this period, except in the structure of the government. At first, the government was in the hands of a *pasha* (governor) and a few high military officers, all from Turkey and appointed by the head of the Ottoman Empire. This system, however, lasted only until 1590. At that time the Turkish occupation army mutinied, massacred the officers in power, and replaced them with new officers who were called *deys*. One of the deys became head of the government and the position of pasha became only an honorary one.

Trade and contact with foreign countries that had begun under the Hafsids continued during the first fifty years of the deys' rule, as a result of a new wave of Moslem and Jewish immigrants who came to Tunisia early in the seventeenth century. Foreign trade with the Middle East and Europe was particularly active during this period, and most of the people accepted the rule of the Turks.

The Turkish government was so firm that it was able to collect taxes regularly throughout the empire. Tax collection was a duty of special army officers known as *beys*. One of these beys, Murad Bey,

acquired enough power during his service to become pasha in 1631. He made the title of pasha important again, and his descendants kept both titles. The deys, in their turn, slowly became mere honorary figures.

In 1702 the Murad dynasty was overthrown and its members massacred by Ibrahim Sharif, an army officer. Sharif then took power and became the first of many rulers to hold the three titles of pasha, dey, and bey. Though Tunisia was still supposed to be part of the Ottoman Empire, for all practical purposes Ibrahim Sharif was an absolute ruler. The head of the Ottoman Empire made no attempt to take away any of his power.

Sharif's successor, Husayn ibn-Ali, came into power in 1710. He was also an army officer and was the first member of

PHOTO TAP TUNIS

the Husainite dynasty. The last member of this dynasty was Lamine Bey, who ruled Tunisia from 1943 to 1957. From 1881 on, however, the rule of the Husainite dynasty was purely honorary. Real power was in the hands of the French.

THE LAST FOREIGN OVERLORD

In the middle of the nineteenth century, Tunisia was experiencing great political, social, and financial difficulties. The government had been building new road and sanitation systems, palaces, and telegraph installations, and creating a new navy. Although some of these programs were useful, they proved to be too costly. Attempts were made to increase taxes, but these attempts led to widespread revolts.

During this period, the major powers in Europe began to take increasing interest in the continent of Africa. Sometimes more than one European nation was interested in a particular area and this created conflict. In 1878 at the Congress of Berlin, the interested European powers divided the African continent among themselves. France, who had extensive investments in Tunis and who had loaned substantial money to the beys, acquired Tunisia and was encouraged to develop its interests there.

In 1881 the French armed forces moved into Tunisia and Ahmed Bey, the ruler then, did not have enough military strength to resist the invasion. He had no alternative but to sign a treaty giving France the right to manage the internal and external affairs of the country.

Left: These cannons once defended Monastir from attacking ships.
Below: The French built large harbors at Bizerte.

The ruling bey signed the Treaty of Bardo in 1881, giving France the right to manage Tunisia's affairs.

Although the treaty allowed the beys to continue to be the official heads of government, the beys could do nothing without the approval of the French resident-general appointed by the French government in Paris.

The French protectorate lasted from 1881 until 1956. Some of its effects have become permanent features of Tunisian life, and the French probably influenced the country as deeply as the Arabs had done twelve centuries earlier. Tunisia's development had remained practically at a standstill from the seventeenth century onward, though progress in every field had been made in Europe. The French colonists brought some of that progress to Tunisia. They built modern highways and railway systems, an airport in Tunis, and large harbors in Tunis, Bizerte, Sousse, and Sfax. They developed the mining industry, agriculture, and trade. The French also created the form of Tunisia's central and local administration and government that still exists today.

Perhaps their most important contribution, and the one that had the greatest effect on Tunisia, was the development of education. Before 1881 there were only small Moslem schools, located usually in or near the mosque (place of worship). Islamic subjects were practically the only ones taught in these schools. Under the French protectorate, modern schools such as those that exist today were built in all major cities. There were, however, two kinds of schools: one kind was exclusively for children of French colonists and was an exact duplicate of schools found in France. French was the only language of instruction in these schools. The second kind of school was reserved for Tunisian children. Part of the instruction was in Arabic and the rest was in French. The lessons were similar to those of the French schools. Thus, French language and culture were brought to Tunisia. Today French is spoken by every educated Tunisian and is the main language of instruction in high schools and at the University of Tunis.

Very few, if any, of France's actions helped the Tunisian population as a whole, nor were they designed to do so. Even though there were schools for Tunisian children, only a small minority of these children attended them. The most important businesses were owned by French businessmen, while the rich farmland of the north was distributed to French farmers. Thus, France's actions were designed to serve its interests first and those of Tunisia only incidentally.

EARLY NATIONALIST MOVEMENTS

Though the Tunisians profited from the presence of the French, the gains they made seemed insignificant when compared with the manner in which the French colonists lived. This situation prompted the Tunisians to organize nationalist movements as early as the 1920s. Early Tunisian nationalism was not a struggle for independence nor was it a movement to eliminate every idea that had come from the French. The early nationalists simply wanted more opportunities for Tunisians under the French system. They were pleased with French culture and language but wanted it made available to more Tunisians. They also wanted Tunisians to become French citizens.

In 1920 the first Tunisian political party was born. It was called the Destour (which means "constitution") and its members came mostly from wealthy Moslem families. The party wanted a constitutional government under the bey, along with greater equality between Frenchmen and Tunisians. The party also favored cooperation with France to achieve these goals.

HABIB BOURGUIBA

The Great Depression of 1929, which hurt almost every country in the world, hit Tunisia very hard. France, which was itself strongly affected by the Great Depression, could neither provide help nor suppress the rising unrest in its colony. It was at this point that Habib Bourguiba entered the political scene.

Born on August 3, 1903, Bourguiba was the eighth and youngest child of a modest family from Monastir. He was able to attend the best high school in Tunis. After graduating, he received a scholarship to study law in Paris. As with many nationalist leaders, Bourguiba found inspiration and ideas for his struggle against colonialism in his French education. While in

school he began to read books and pamphlets by French thinkers and philosophers of the eighteenth and nineteenth centuries. These men exalted the ideas of human freedom and equality.

In 1927 Bourguiba returned to Tunis where he opened a law office. Although he had joined the Destour Party in 1922, he did not become active in it until 1930. At that time he began publishing highly nationalistic newspaper articles, in which he accused the French of being responsible for the misery and extreme poverty of most of Tunisia. In 1934 he and his followers split from the Destour Party, which they thought was not moving ahead quickly enough, to form their own Néo-Destour (New Destour) Party.

The new party, whose slogan was "Freedom with Bourguiba," quickly attracted a following of people who had never participated in politics before; many of these people were small businessmen and farmers. The French realized that this new party was a serious threat to them, and they banned it less than eight months after it was started. They also jailed all of its leaders, including Bourguiba. This was the beginning of a struggle which involved Bourguiba and his Néo-Destour Party, the French settlers in Tunisia, and the French government in Paris. The struggle lasted twenty-one years. During this period, each succeeding colonial administration established different policies toward Tunisia. One administration gave way to the nationalists' pressure and granted them some concessions, while another favored the French settlers and used force and oppression against the nationalists.

INDEPENDENCE

After World War II Bourguiba became even more influential and the people grew tired of the French policies. In 1953 many incidents of armed resistance against the French resulted in a period of serious tension. The French, who were just then extracting themselves from a costly war in Indochina, finally gave in. On March 20, 1956 Tunisia became an independent nation.

Five days later the first elections were held. Supporters of Habib Bourguiba won by a large majority. A Constituent Assembly was chosen to draft a constitution for the country. On April 8 the Assembly held its first meeting. At that time Bourguiba was elected president of the Assembly and proceeded to pass a series of resolutions which the bey signed. In these resolutions the bey gave up most of his powers. On July 25 the Assembly voted to abolish the monarchy and to replace it with a republic. Bourguiba became temporary president of the republic until the constitution was drafted and approved.

Arab children at school. The French established separate schools for French and Arabs.

Tunisia Today

POSTINDEPENDENCE PROBLEMS

At the time of independence, Tunisia had all the problems that are common to underdeveloped countries. There was practically no industry or manufacturing, the country's agriculture was not mechanized and could not feed the total population, and very few local people were educated. Earnings from the country's two major exports—olive oil and phosphate—were rarely sufficient to pay for the amount of food imports needed. Furthermore, health care and education were not available for all.

Another major problem that Bourguiba and his government had to face in 1957 was the dominant role that the French played in the country's daily life. Banks, offices, major stores, post offices, communication and transportation systems, schools, and even government agencies were all run by French officials. The government, however, could not immediately ask them to leave, for without them the whole country would come to a halt. There were not enough qualified Tunisians to replace the French.

Between 1958 and 1964, relations between Tunisia and France went from friendly cooperation to sudden, violent conflict. Tunisia knew it still had to rely quite heavily on France, but at the same time it did not want to allow France to

At independence Tunisia's agriculture was not mechanized. Here a farmer mows a field of clover in the traditional way.

AID

47

threaten its newly acquired independence. Tunisia had conceded to France the temporary right to maintain military bases in Bizerte and the Sahara. The two countries agreed to discuss later what would happen to the French businesses and farms, including large acreages of land occupied by French settlers.

ALGERIA AND BIZERTE

Tunisia was able to achieve independence without much violence but its neighbor, Algeria, was not so fortunate. Beginning in November of 1954, Algeria fought a full-scale war against the French. Tunisia felt obligated to help Algeria in its fight for independence since Algeria was a neighbor and they had similar goals. Thus, the Algerian freedom fighters were allowed to use Tunisian soil as a base from which they could launch attacks on the French army in Algeria. President Bourguiba declared in 1959, "Tunisia will not allow France to use our country as a rear base in the war she is waging in Algeria."

These policies did not please France, who warned Tunisia not to give refuge to the Algerian soldiers. When Tunisia continued to do so, France first cut off its aid, then threatened to call back to France French civilians on whom Tunisia depended greatly to keep its government and economy functioning smoothly.

The most drastic action came on February 8, 1958, when the French air force bombed Sakiet-Sidi-Youssef, a small Tunisian village on the Algerian border that was supposed to be a stronghold of Algerian fighters. The bombing resulted in the total destruction of the town and the death of a large number of civilians. It became clear to the Tunisians that they would never achieve total independence from the French without violence and bloodshed, and Bourguiba declared that every sacrifice would be made in order to evacuate all French armed forces from Tunisian soil.

Shortly after the incident at Sakiet-Sidi-Youssef, the government of the French Fourth Republic fell. The government was reorganized and General Charles de Gaulle, a leader in the French World War II resistance against the Germans, came to power as the first president of the Fifth Republic. De Gaulle immediately agreed to evacuate all the French military bases in Tunisia, except the one in Bizerte. This was a great step forward, but still short of Tunisia's goal of total evacuation.

The final showdown over Bizerte came in July of 1961. At that time, the French were lengthening an airstrip at the base, although they had signed an agreement not to extend their military facilities in any way without prior permission from the Tunisian government. The Tunisian government officially protested to Paris, but when construction did not stop, Tunisian soldiers surrounded the base. The supply of food for the French soldiers was cut off. The battle lasted for three days; the French used planes and parachutists from Algeria. Hundreds of Tunisians were killed and nearly the whole town of Bizerte was occupied by the French.

CEASE FIRE

On July 23, a cease fire was ordered by the Security Council of the United Nations (UN). On the following day, Dag Hammarskjöld, then the UN secretary-general, came to Tunisia to investigate the Bizerte situation. For over a month after the cease fire, Tunisian diplomats traveled all over the world trying to win support for their cause. These efforts were successful; on August 27 the UN General Assembly, meeting for the first time ever in a previously unplanned session, passed a resolution ordering France out of Bizerte. Two-thirds of the members voted for the resolution, one-third abstained (did not vote), and not a single member voted against it. This move was a major victory for Tunisia, but it took a long time for the French to carry out the resolution. It was

Old women at an Algerian refugee camp near Le Kef eat wild vegetation for food.

not until 1963, more than two years later, that the last French soldier left Tunisia.

This, however, was not the end of conflict between France and Tunisia. Most of the rich land of northern Tunisia was still held by French settlers, and the Tunisian government wanted to buy back that land. Knowing that they were eventually going to lose the land, the settlers stopped working it and caring for it properly. Consequently, the government decided to nationalize (take over) the land before it was badly damaged. On May 12, 1964, exactly eighty-three years after Tunisia had become a French protectorate, President Bourguiba signed the nationalization law. Once again, relations between France and Tunisia became strained.

President de Gaulle, however, was eager to end all French colonial involvements and at the same time keep the friendship of France's former colonies. After the initial furor over nationalization ended, the two governments negotiated a satisfactory settlement to all disputes between them. Now that the last traces of colonialism were gone and independence was finally felt to be real and complete, Tunisia turned its energies to the development of its own society.

A MODERN NATION

Tunisia has acquired an international reputation as a serious, hardworking nation. Many people consider its president, Habib Bourguiba, a great twentieth century leader. The late President John F. Kennedy referred to Bourguiba as the "George Washington of Tunisia." In 1961 a Tunisian diplomat named Mongi Slim was elected president of the UN General Assembly, an important honor for a new nation. Since then, many Tunisian leaders have acted as mediators between disagreeing nations in Africa and the Middle East.

Tunisia receives economic aid from countries all over the world. That aid has been used to start new industries and to modernize agriculture. Tunisia was also fortunate because unlike many other newly independent African and Moslem nations, Tunisia did not experience a single revolution or violent upheaval of any consequence. Second, Tunisia is one of the few countries to have a program of population control—the first of its kind in a Moslem country. Without this, economic progress would have been wiped out by a quickly rising population.

Unfortunately, much of what had been so painfully achieved since independence was wiped out by the terrible floods of 1969. Torrential rains fell throughout Tunisia for four consecutive days, beginning on September 25. At the end of the rain, at least five hundred people had been killed by the flooding. Over one hundred thousand houses had been swept away or destroyed, along with hundreds of miles of roads and telephone lines. Fifty bridges had been destroyed when the streams they spanned suddenly became furious rivers. The flood turned all of southern Tunisia into a gigantic lake.

Because of this disaster, Tunisia's economic development was set back five years. The entire country mobilized to help the disaster area. Money and personnel came from all over the world, by way of UN agencies or directly from sympathetic countries.

THE GOVERNMENT OF TUNISIA

The constitution of Tunisia was passed by Tunisia's Constituent Assembly on May 28, 1959 and put into effect four days later. The first article of the constitution proclaims that "Tunisia shall be a free, independent and sovereign state, Islamic in religion, Arabic in language and republican in regime." Although the constitution calls for the creation of three separate governmental branches—executive, legislative, and judicial—it clearly gives much more power to the executive than to the other two branches. Aside from the powers that presidents usually have, such as appointing government officials, heading the armed forces, and enforcing laws—the Tunisian president has the right to initiate laws that the legislature must consider first, to make official decrees that have the effect of laws, and even to

This train crash was caused by the collapse of a bridge, due to great flooding in 1969.

propose changes to the constitution in every way except abolishing the republican regime.

The president also appoints a cabinet consisting of twelve ministers responsible for such areas as the interior and the treasury. The president is elected for a five-year term and is not eligible for more than three successive terms. He must also be a native Tunisian, a Moslem, and at least forty years old.

Unlike the chief executives of most countries, the president of Tunisia is in close contact with his people. When he comes to work, many people wait to see him. Sometimes these people hand him letters asking for a favor or informing him of a problem. The president usually accepts these letters personally.

The legislative branch is *unicameral,* or made up of one house. This body is called the National Assembly. It has ninety members called *deputies,* who are elected directly by the people eligible to vote. This system of election is called *direct universal suffrage.* The members of the Assembly hold five-year terms, and the constitution declares that "every deputy in the National Assembly shall be considered as representing the whole nation." This system is different from the American system, where each senator and representative represents only a certain state or area.

The president and the deputies must be elected at the same time and by free, direct, and secret voting open to all citizens at least twenty years of age.

The Assembly meets for two sessions a year, each session not longer than three months. The Assembly must ratify the national budget, which is written by the executive branch of government. So far, the National Assembly has not been very important in politics, which has been dominated by the executive branch.

The judicial branch is quite different from that of the United States. There is no Supreme Court with the power of reviewing laws to determine whether they fit the requirements of the constitution. Civil and criminal judges are appointed by the president, but the constitution does not specify whether they can be dismissed, under what circumstances, and by whom.

Tunisia is a *unitary* state; that is, all power is in the hands of the central national government. To make it easier to govern, however, the country is divided into 13 *wilayat* (governorates), each headed by a *wali* (governor). The wilayat are in turn divided into 97 *mutamadiyat* (regions). These are divided further into 750 *shaykhat* (localities). The local officials are not elected but are appointed and can be dismissed by the president of the republic upon recommendation from the Minister of the Interior.

There is only one political party in Tunisia, the Socialist Destour Party (PSD), headed by Bourguiba. It replaced the old Néo-Destour Party. Most members of the government are also members of the PSD, and candidates for elective offices must generally run on this party's ticket in order to be elected.

TUNISIA
GOVERNORATES

TRANSPORTATION AND COMMUNICATION

In 1881 Tunisia's highway system consisted of a two-and-one-half mile, stone-covered road connecting Tunis to the king's palace in the suburb of Bardo. There were some dirt roads and remains of the highways that the Romans had built. When the protectorate was established, the French authorities made no attempt at first to build roads, because efforts were concentrated on constructing a railroad system. Between 1878 and 1900, the railroads were used mostly for the transportation of minerals from the interior to the harbors; practically no passengers used the trains.

The French carefully planned the railroad system in a practical, economical manner. It consisted of a main north-south line running from Tunis to Gabès and of secondary branches running in an east-west direction. The network has remained virtually unchanged, and its total length is exactly 1,243 miles.

After World War I, people began to use automobiles more and more. Thus, the construction of modern highways was necessary. By 1940 the French had built about two thousand miles of surfaced roads, most of which paralleled the railroad tracks. By 1950 the system was increased to a total of about fifty-five hundred miles, with some thirty-five hundred miles of dirt roads. Since independence, more new roads have been built, and today there are about four thousand miles of surfaced roads, with eight thousand additional miles of dirt roads. The government is in the process of converting the dirt roads to all-weather roads.

Tunisia's strategic location in North Africa makes it a convenient refueling stop for planes connecting Africa with the Middle East and Europe. In 1945 an airport and a modern airfield were built near Tunis. By 1965 the Tunis airport was handling seventy-three hundred flights and more than three hundred thousand passengers per year. As more and more tourists visited Tunisia, those figures increased by more than 10 percent every year. The government has built new facilities to handle the increased traffic and the bigger jets. A new airport was recently constructed with American aid. It began operation in 1973. In addition, there are two other international airports in operation, in Monastir and on the island of Djerba; both of these have direct flights to Europe. The government owns and operates an airline called Tunis-Air.

There are four major national newspapers in Tunisia, two of which—one in Arabic and one in French—are published

by the PSD. In addition, many European newspapers and magazines are sold. The United States, France, England, and Germany also have widely used information centers in Tunisia where books and periodicals are available.

The Tunisian government operates the national radio and television network. Television was introduced in 1965 and has become very popular; though there were only three thousand sets in use in 1965, there were fifty thousand sets in 1970. Broadcasts are in French and Arabic, and newly built relay towers allow viewers in Tunis to watch programs from France, Italy, Algeria, and Libya.

There are fewer than fifty thousand telephones in the country, but the government is trying to meet the great demands for this service. Thanks to a direct line with Paris, telephone communications are possible with most countries.

Left: This jeep is halted as camels cross the road. Below: Men on the dock at the port of Mahdia listen as one reads an Arabic newspaper aloud.

A group of men take time off from work for an outdoor lesson.

TEACHING AND LEARNING

Under the French protectorate, the children of French settlers were all educated, but only about 10 percent of school-age Tunisian children were able to go to school. Since almost none of them went beyond the primary level, in 1956 only 16 percent of the total population knew how to read or write.

Another problem was that most of the people viewed life in the traditional Moslem way, and it was hard for them to adapt to the ways of the twentieth century. For example, most parents refused to allow their daughters to go to school, because they believed that it was evil for a woman to work outside the home or even to be out on the street.

President Bourguiba declared at the time of independence that every Tunisian not only had the right to education but also had the duty to go to school to help turn Tunisia into a modern nation. From 1956 on, the government has spent between one-fourth and one-third of the annual

*A first grade
student does
his lesson on
the blackboard
at school.*

PHOTO TAP. TUNIS

national budget for education. Tunisia is one of the few countries in the world that has spent such a large percentage of its budget on educating its people. The government also took over control of two hundred Islamic schools, and the distinction between religious and public schools was ended.

The University of Tunis was founded in 1959 and consisted of a few buildings scattered around the city of Tunis. In 1970 it was moved to a new site in a suburb and equipped with the latest research facilities and scientific equipment. Now the university trains not only Tunisians but students from all over Africa.

Today the results of the government's educational efforts are quite impressive. After fifteen years of independence, the number of school students has increased greatly.

The educational system in existence today is practically the same as the one used in France except that school is taught in both Arabic and French. There are six years of primary school, seven of secondary school, and four at the university level. To go from one level to another, students must pass national exams. Before each exam is given, the Minister of Education estimates the number of vacancies in the schools and only that many people will pass the exams. If a person reaches the university level, he must pass exams every year to continue from one year to the next. Students are usually expelled if they fail a particular year's exams more than twice. After four years at the university, students may continue on for a graduate degree.

Since the government of Tunisia wants everyone to know how to read and write, most of the new schools are primary schools. New schools are being built everywhere, particularly in areas where not very many people live. Throughout the countryside are small school buildings that seem to sit in the middle of nowhere, miles away from any town or village. These schools have one or two classrooms and a small apartment where the teacher lives. The teacher not only teaches, but also acts as the principal, administrator, and janitor. These schools were built for children whose parents are small farmers or nomads.

In 1971 only 76 percent of school-age children attended school, and about 68 percent of the total population was still illiterate. Most of these people were adults who had not been able to attend school under the protectorate. Now they attend special adult classes, which are organized in every community. People come in large numbers to learn reading, writing, and mathematics, as well as civics, new farming techniques, and other subjects.

Reading and writing is not enough, though. Tunisia also needs trained people to work in factories, shops, offices, and hospitals. Because building schools is very expensive, on the average only about 40 percent of the primary-level students are able to continue on to secondary school. The other students must return to their villages or go to the cities where they try to make a living by finding taxis for people, selling nuts on the beaches, or shining shoes. More often than not, these people slowly become illiterate again, forgetting everything they learned in school.

Those who do attend secondary school usually want an education that will make it easy for them to get a clerical or office job. Those who intend to go on to a university usually plan to study such subjects as law, literature, and languages, though the country badly needs people qualified for technical jobs. Consequently, there are too many secondary-school graduates who are qualified for administrative jobs and not enough who are qualified for the important technical jobs.

Through scholarships, the government has tried to encourage people to study technical subjects. Many of those who fail exams in the regular secondary courses enroll in the technical courses. The government guarantees jobs to those who finish their studies.

Natural Treasures

MINERAL TREASURES

Tunisia's most important mineral resource is phosphates, which are made into fertilizer at the cities of Sfax and Gafsa and exported. Today Tunisia is the world's third largest exporter of phosphates. Production increased dramatically from about two hundred thousand tons at independence to three million tons in 1971.

There are also large iron ore deposits along the Algerian borders. These deposits are very close to the surface, making open-pit mining possible. The ore is very rich in iron content. Production of iron ore stood at 850,000 tons in 1971, having increased from 117,500 tons in 1956. In the past about 80 percent of the iron ore was exported. In the last few years, however, the mineral has all been used by the new steel mill at Menzel Bourguiba.

Other mineral resources exist in Tunisia, including lead, zinc, and silver. Of these, lead is the most important, for fourteen thousand tons of it are exported each year.

Tunisia's greatest hope for future mineral wealth is oil. In 1965 an important oil field was discovered south of Gabès. This discovery encouraged many oil companies to prospect for oil throughout Tunisia and along the eastern coast. Deposits have been found near Sfax and off the shores of the Island of Kerkenna.

ANIMAL TREASURES

Seals are usually found only in cold climates like that of the Arctic Circle, but there is a small, rocky island about fifty miles from Tabarka, which has a large population of these animals. No one knows why these cold-climate animals live on the Mediterranean Sea.

More expected in North Africa is the camel, and Tunisia has many of them. Camels are used in the Sahara for transportation as well as for working the land and drawing water from wells. The milk of the female camel is used as a staple food by the Bedouins and other nomadic people, much as people in temperate climates use milk from cows or goats. The camel can go for weeks without water and with very little food and can travel up to

Camels rest and drink water at an oasis in the Sahara.

forty miles a day; it is sometimes called "the ship of the desert." For many centuries, camels were used exclusively to carry goods between North Africa, the Middle East, and central and southern Africa. Today camels are still widely used throughout southern Tunisia.

In the desert live not only camels, but also many small animals that are often very deadly. Among these are varieties of dangerous snakes, scorpions, spiders, and lizards.

Tunisia's waters are very rich in all kinds of sea animals, including tuna, sardine, octopus, lobster, and crab. Oyster and mussel beds are found near Bizerte, and sponges are harvested off the coasts of Sfax and the island of Djerba.

Except for wild boars in the north and gazelles in the south, there are very few big wild animals in Tunisia.

GROWING THINGS

The lovely little fill is a small flower found in only a few other countries in the world. It is white and only about an inch long, with a hollow stem and a strong, sweet smell. The fill is gathered for small bouquets, in which each flower is stuck on the end of a dry blade of alfa grass to form what Tunisians called a *mashmum*. During the summertime, people often buy mashmums and wear them behind their right ears.

Similar to the fill and cultivated in many parts of the country is the jasmine. This flower also has a prominent scent and is used to make perfumes and tea. Other flowers found in Tunisia include the small but very fragrant Arabic rose, carnations, lilies, and several types of shrubs.

Just as the cactus is associated with the American desert, alfa grass is associated with the Sahara. Alfa grass grows naturally in most of southern Tunisia, usually in small bushes about three feet high and light brown in color. It is normally used as camel feed, but recently paper has been manufactured from it. The desert also has a type of cactus with thick leaves about a foot long and covered with thorns. This cactus produces a fruit known as barbary figs, called *hindee* in Tunisia.

Aside from the olive tree, which is considered by many Tunisian peasants as a symbol of wealth, the palm tree is perhaps the most characteristic tree of the country. Since palms need plenty of sun but little water to grow, they are found in large numbers in the south. The entire tree is useful. Palms produce a liquid called *legmee,* a very popular drink in Tunisia. When the legmee is fermented, it becomes a kind of wine. The leaves of the trees are used to make baskets and their trunks to make roofs for homes.

Because Tunisia lacks trees for wood and because there is widespread erosion due to the brief but heavy rains, the government has begun a program to plant hardwood trees throughout the country. There is even a "tree day" each year on which the president and other members of the government plant trees and encourage the rest of the population to do likewise.

The People Live in Tunisia

THE BERBERS TODAY

The Berbers were the original inhabitants of Tunisia and made up the majority of the population for many centuries. Today very few Tunisians are of pure Berber blood and still retain the Berber language and culture. The exact number of pure Berbers is not known but is probably less than fifty thousand of the country's five million inhabitants. These people are concentrated in the northeast, the southwest near Gafsa, and on the island of Djerba. Many of them have blond or red hair and blue or green eyes, and all of them speak the Berber language. Language, however, will soon cease to separate the Berbers from the rest of the country, since more and more young Berbers are brought up speaking both Arabic and Berber.

OTHER ETHNIC GROUPS

All of Tunisia's minority groups together make up only two percent of the population. For a long time there was a large Jewish community in Tunisia, concentrated on the island of Djerba, in Tunis, and in some of the northern cities. The majority of these people were shopkeepers, businessmen, and skilled craftsmen. Though a number of them left after independence, the ones who remained worked and lived as they always had and practiced their religion freely.

A student who arrived at school early reads while waiting for the doors to open.

ABDELHAMID KAHIA, A I D

63

Above: An impoverished family squats on the ground. Left: This woman's kitchen is outside her house. Opposite top: A Berber man. Opposite right: Young and old shop at the souk. Opposite bottom: Children sit in the sun on their rural dwelling.

ABDELHAMID KAHIA. A I D

Before 1956 there were more than two hundred thousand Europeans living in Tunisia. Though most were French citizens, a few were Italian, Maltese, Spanish, or Greek. Many of the French were government officials, businessmen, or farmers, but most of them had left the country after independence and the nationalization of all foreign-held lands. Today there are very few Frenchmen left in Tunisia; most of them and the other Europeans have been hired to work as teachers, doctors, and technicians.

There are a few blacks in Tunisia, mostly the descendants of slaves who were being taken across the Sahara but who somehow escaped and settled at the desert oases.

There are also a few people who are thought to be pure Arabs, direct descendants of the Beni Hilal and other Arab invaders of the eleventh century. They are scattered in southern and central Tunisia, particularly around the city of Kairouan, and are divided into clans, or groups of many related families. The most famous clan is the Zlass, who organize a great annual festival known as *fantasia*. During this time, the Zlass dress as warriors and simulate a battle during which they exhibit their skills on horseback.

MODERN VS. TRADITIONAL LIFE

The majority of the population is basically of Berber ancestry, mixed to some extent with other nationalities. In language and religion, however, the country is completely Arab. Very few countries have such a homogeneous population; this homogeneity of the population is the prime reason why Tunisia has not had ethnic or religious wars, as have so many other African countries.

The divisions that do exist in Tunisian society are between the urban and the rural people, and between the modern and traditional ways of life. Two out of three Tunisians either live in small villages or are Bedouin nomads who have no permanent home. These people have little or no education and grow only enough food to feed themselves. They live just as their ancestors did and do not want to adopt such modern customs as going to school, using mechanical farming techniques, or taking modern medicines when they are ill.

The other one-third of Tunisia's population lives in towns and cities. In many ways they are similar to people living in American and European cities. They want to go to school and especially want to improve their way of life. Many of these people have been to foreign countries, and all of them come into regular contact with books, magazines, plays, movies, and radio. They are not as interested in maintaining tradition as are the rural people; they want the society around them to become more modern.

Sometimes these two classes of people come into direct conflict with each other. The Koran (Moslem holy book), for example, says that all Moslems must fast every day from sunrise to sundown during the entire month of Ramadan, which occurs in the autumn. During that time, people usually do not have enough energy to work as much as they normally do, and business slows down during that month. Thus, President Bourguiba urged his people not to fast. He said that Islam allows people not to fast when they are waging a battle and argued that the Tunisians are engaged in a battle against underdevelopment. He then drank a glass of orange juice in public. This move created quite an uproar, and the protest was so great that Bourguiba announced that he would leave it up to each individual to decide whether or not to fast.

WOMEN

Because of religious laws and social customs, Tunisian women were considered second-class citizens until recently. All women wore veils, allowing only their eyes to show, and were not allowed outside their homes except to work on family farms. They had no civil rights, received no education, and had no voice in their own private lives. Before marriage, a girl was under her father's authority. After she married the man her father chose for her, the authority was simply transferred to the husband. If she lived in the country, she did almost all the work in the fields, in addition to the work at home. Men, however, were allowed to have as many as four wives at the same time and could divorce any of them by simply telling them to go back to their father's home. There was nothing the women could do about it.

After independence, however, this situation changed. Today, by law, women are full citizens, with the same rights and duties as men. They can vote, run for office, hold jobs, and are responsible for their own finances. Many of the younger women no longer wear the veil that their mothers wore. Thousands of girls attend schools, and many more hold jobs and are active outside the home. Divorce is carried out in the courts and almost no man has more than one wife.

The relationships between men and women, however, are not yet as free as they are in Europe and in the United States. For example, most parents still do not allow their daughters to date boys or even to socialize with them and often still insist that girls marry someone the parents choose. These traditions will probably become more relaxed over the course of time.

DRESS AND CUSTOMS

Although many Tunisian men and women wear the same type of clothes that Europeans and Americans do, traditional dress is still very common throughout the countryside. For men, traditional dress is a wide robe—usually white or grey—with a V-opening in front from the neck to the waist. This robe is called a *jebba*, and the small, red hat worn with it is called a *chechia*. Another common garment, the *blousa,* is similar to the jebba but is much smaller. In addition to the jebba, men in rural areas sometimes wear a *burnous,* a large cape with a hood, and replace the chechia with a turban.

Traditional dress for women tends to vary from the cities to the countryside. Traditional city dress is a *futa-wa-blusa,* which is a long, sleeveless dress. In the street a *safsari* is worn. This is a large piece of cloth made out of silk with which women cover themselves from head to toe, leaving only a small opening for the eyes. Safsaris are different from region to region. Rural women wear a short shirt called a *surya* or *kamezuna* and on top of it a long, multicolored piece of cloth known as a *malia.* They also cover their hair with a scarf, but do not wear a safsari.

THE ARTS

Because dancing used to be considered sinful by Moslems, only slaves and concubines would dance. Today, however, belly dancing is very popular in Tunisia and throughout the Middle East.

Many professional Tunisian dancers visit villages in the interior of the country to observe how the women dance. Then they try to teach and perform these dances in an attempt to preserve them. The National Folkloric Troupe is the best known dance group in Tunisia.

Theater is also very popular in Tunisia. Performers from Tunis and from all over Europe appear regularly in the magnificent Tunis Municipal Theater.

A Tunisian dancer performs a dance with jugs.

Tunisians are very fond of movies. In addition to the many theaters that show movies from Europe, the United States, and Egypt, there are a few theaters that show special films.

CUISINE

No tourist ever leaves Tunisia without sampling some of the country's traditional dishes. The most famous dish is *kusksee,* which is ground wheat cooked in steam heat and mixed with a sauce made of lamb and various vegetables. An especially popular salad is *slata-mashuya,* which consists of tomatoes, green peppers, and onions broiled over an open fire, cut in small pieces, and mixed with olive oil, tuna, and spices. Another Tunisian specialty is *breek*, a very thin sheet of dough filled with mashed potatoes, ground meat, an egg, and herbs and spices, then fried in olive oil. Tunisians often challenge foreigners to eat the breek without spilling the egg, which is usually left soft. Fish is very popular in Tunisia and is prepared in many different ways.

RELIGION

The Islamic religion originated in Arabia (today known as Saudi Arabia). At the time Islam began, Arabia was populated by nomadic peoples, many of whom were traders carrying goods back and forth between Asia and the Middle East. One such group of people was called Beni Hashim, and among them was a woman named Amina. She gave birth in 571 to a boy who was given the name of Mohammed. Her husband, Abdallah, had died shortly before the baby was born and when Amina died six years later, the boy went to live with his grandfather. When the grandfather also died, Mohammed went to live with his uncle, a rich trader who took him along on his travels. Mohammed learned the trader's skills, married a rich widow who owned caravans, and opened his own business.

One night when Mohammed was thirty-nine years old, he went for one of his frequent walks to the hills near Mecca. There was a cave where he liked to sit and meditate. That night he suddenly heard a voice ordering him to read. Mohammed was frightened and as he looked around him, he saw the archangel Jibril (Gabriel) holding out a parchment. "But I don't know how to read," answered Mohammed. "Read in the name of thy God the Almighty," said Jibril. This was the Night of Destiny, during which the angel Jibril revealed to Mohammed the first verses of the Koran (Qur'an), the holy book of the Moslems. Mohammed learned from Jibril on this night that he, Mohammed, was to be God's messenger on earth—the prophet of Islam.

Thus Islam began. Mohammed began preaching the new religion in Mecca. At first no one took him seriously, but when his followers—mostly the poor and disadvantaged—grew in number, the rich merchants began showing much hostility toward him. In 622 the danger became so great that the prophet had to flee to Medina (Madina), another town in Arabia. That year marks the beginning of the Moslem calendar.

Most of the laws and principles of Islam are found in the Koran. Every Moslem must practice the so-called "Five Pillars of Islam." These are: to accept that there is no god but Allah and that Mohammed is his prophet; to pray five times a day; to fast every day during the month of Ramadan from sunrise to sunset; to give alms to the poor; and to go on pilgrimage to Mecca at least once in one's lifetime, if possible. The Koran also contains the rules that guide the daily life of Moslems.

This was the religion that Mohammed's descendants and followers took to the confines of Asia and to Europe at a speed and with a success unmatched by any other religion. The Moslem Arabs settled in Tunisia in 670 and quickly dominated North Africa.

HOUSING AND HEALTH

Many people from rural areas come to the cities each year to find work. Not only do they usually have few skills, but they always have had trouble finding decent places to live. They used to live in slums called *bidonvilles*, which were so named because the houses were made of mud and covered with *bidons* (gasoline barrels) flattened to form metal sheets. Today the larger bidonvilles have been torn down, but many smaller ones still exist on the outskirts of Tunis and other major cities. The government plans to eliminate all the bidonvilles and construct new housing for these immigrants. The people are being provided with free construction materials, loans, and grants. They are also encouraged to form housing cooperatives; each of the tenants owns a part of the cooperative housing development. The government also builds thousands of

A bidonville in Tunis.

homes every year. Through all these programs, the government hopes to eliminate bidonvilles and other poor housing by the end of the 1970s.

When the French ruled Tunisia, they concentrated their efforts in the cities. The countryside, where most of the population lived, remained poor, uneducated, and without good housing or health facilities. As a result, many serious diseases such as typhus, tuberculosis, and trachoma spread throughout the country, killing large numbers of people every year.

After independence the government initiated a comprehensive program to correct that situation. The Ministry of Public Health now has a budget of more than ten million dollars, the third largest budget in the government. Inoculations against different diseases are administered free of charge to children in schools, and mobile units travel throughout the country to provide the same service. Over 450 small clinics and first aid centers have been built; here people are treated and taught how to take better care of themselves. In addition, there are 82 modern and well-equipped hospitals where treatment is given free to those who cannot afford to pay.

The biggest problem in keeping these programs going is that there is a severe shortage of doctors and nurses in Tunisia. There is only about one Tunisian doctor for every ten thousand people and one dentist for every one hundred thousand people. Most of these native doctors have private practices in the major cities. Hundreds of foreign doctors have been brought to Tunisia to help out, and Tunisian doctors are now required to spend part of their time working in public hospitals and to accept assignments in rural areas.

Today the country is free of major diseases. There are no completely undernourished people, but many people still eat mostly starches and carbohydrates and not enough protein and vitamins. This is partly because the people do not know which foods are best for them. To teach them about nutrition, the government has recently begun using radio, television, and newspapers. Since nearly everyone in the country sees or hears at least one of these forms of media regularly, nutrition is expected to improve in the near future.

One result of the successful health program has been a dramatic increase in the size of the population. The birth rate was always high, but many children died when they were very young because their parents did not know what to do about their illnesses. Now medical care has improved greatly and in the fifteen years after independence, the population has increased by 45 percent.

This rate of increase is too high. If it continues, there will be too many people and not enough food, jobs, or medicine. Thus, the government has sought help, especially from the United Nations and the United States, to teach people about family planning so that the population growth will slow down. Tunisia was the first Arab country to adopt such a policy, and it seems to be successful.

The People Work in Tunisia

In 1971 Tunisia's work force was made up of only half of the people in the country. Fifty percent of these people were engaged in agriculture, fishing, and mining, 20 percent in industry, and 30 percent in what is called the *tertiary sector*—service industries such as tourism, transportation, medicine, and education.

Most of the agricultural workers in Tunisia have few skills, if any. They are constantly migrating around the country looking for jobs. Some of them are hired as sharecroppers to farm a section of land. Sharecroppers are usually paid about a dollar a day, but sometimes they get to keep part of what they grow. The government has been trying to organize these workers and to regulate their salaries, working conditions, and benefits. So far the government has had little success, mainly because the people do not stay in one place very long and because they constantly move in and out of the work force.

Workers in mining and industry, who tend to stay in one job for a long time, have been organized since 1946, when the General Union of Tunisian Workers (UGTT) was formed by Farhat Hached. During the years when the Néo-Destour Party was banned, the UGTT played an important role in the fight for independence. In the early 1950s, the French settlers living in Tunisia were afraid of the power of the UGTT. In an attempt to break it up, they killed the union leader, Hached, in December of 1952. That act made the Tunisian workers even more determined to continue the

A farmer holds a few of the potatoes he has harvested.

fight for independence. Today Hached is considered a national hero and memorial services are held every year to commemorate his death.

The UGTT now has a membership of about 150,000 and about a dozen labor unions are affiliated with it. The UGTT has been under government control since the 1960s, mostly so that major strikes would not disrupt the country. Strikes are illegal, and both the workers and the managers accept all labor laws passed by the government.

In 1960 a social security fund was established in Tunisia. Both workers and employers contribute to this fund. Members are entitled to such benefits as medical care, child support, and maternity allowances.

Another important labor law was passed in 1966. This law set the minimum wage at seventy-five milliemes an hour (equivalent to US $0.14). The work week was set at forty-eight hours. This law also stated that every worker must have twenty-four consecutive hours off each week and periodic rest breaks during working hours. Large employers were also required to have health facilities and to give workers regular medical checkups.

TOURISM

Tunisia's newest major industry is tourism. The mild weather all year round, the hundreds of miles of beaches, interesting archaeological sites, and the appeal of an Arab culture make Tunisia a fascinating place to visit. Until 1962, however, not many people visited Tunisia. At that time the government initiated a wide-ranging program to attract tourists to Tunisia. Information offices were set up throughout Europe and North America to work with travel agencies and to advertise in newspapers and magazines.

At the same time, many hotels were built throughout the country to accommodate the tourists. From a few small hotels with a total capacity of four thousand beds in 1956, Tunisia had nearly two hundred hotels with fifty-four thousand beds in 1971. These hotels are usually more than half filled throughout the year, but during the summer months they are always booked solid. Sometimes reservations must be made as far as two years in advance!

For a long time most visitors to Tunisia were French. Since 1968, however, the Germans have become the largest group of tourists, followed closely by the French, the British, and the Italians. American visitors numbered about three thousand in 1962, but in 1971 more than twelve thousand Americans visited Tunisia. In 1971 a total of 620,000 tourists came to Tunisia and it is expected that in 1980, 1.5 million foreigners will visit the country.

This tremendous expansion has created thousands of new jobs. Aside from the people who build the hotels, many others are needed to operate them. It is estimated that fifteen thousand new jobs have been created in the last ten years as a result of the tourist industry, and two thousand new ones will be created every year during the remainder of the 1970s.

AGRICULTURE

Agriculture is still by far the most important type of work done in Tunisia. Half the population depends on it for a living. Only about 56 percent of the land, however, can be used for agriculture. Of that area, one-fourth is mostly grazing land and 14 percent is covered by forests. This leaves an area of about twenty thousand square miles, or thirteen million acres, that is actually used for farming. About 85 percent of the farms have less than fifty acres, and 41 percent are between three and ten acres in size. The number of small farms makes it difficult to bring modern farm machinery and techniques to Tunisia.

In the past, the average Tunisian peasant owned a small piece of land on which he grew a little wheat and barley, mostly for his own use. He might also have had a few olive trees and perhaps a half dozen sheep and goats. When the rains were plentiful and the crops were good, everyone was happy. If, however, the crops failed for many years, the whole country was affected. The government had to distribute food to keep the people from starving.

Modern combines have aided farmers in cultivating wheat.

AID

A weaver works at his loom.

In the early 1960s the government decided that this state of affairs must be changed. Ahmed Ben Salah, who was then Minister of the Economy, took several steps to alter Tunisian agriculture. He urged farmers to switch to crops, such as fruits and vegetables, that could be irrigated, and give up those that depend entirely on rain. He also moved to combine small farms into large ones by means of cooperatives, so that machinery could be used to raise the output. The peasants, however, did not want to join cooperatives, for they were proud of owning their own farmlands. When the co-ops became compulsory, the peasants refused to work the land. Some even burned their crops, cut down their trees, and slaughtered their livestock. In 1969 the situation became so serious that the government fired Ben Salah and put him on trial for conspiracy against the national interest. The cooperatives were then abolished.

Wheat and barley are the basis of the national diet, but Tunisia also has thirty-two million olive trees that produce about ninety thousand tons of excellent olive oil each year. Two-thirds of Tunisia's olive oil is exported, making Tunisia one of the world's largest exporters of this product. In addition, the 3.2 million palm trees, found mainly in the south, yield several varieties of dates that are very popular in Europe. About five thousand tons of dates are exported every year. Other important agricultural products include ninety-four thousand tons of citrus fruits, mostly grown on the peninsula of Cape Bon; twenty thousand tons of apricots, grown at Sousse and Gabès; and sixty-five thousand tons of almonds. In 1968 twenty thousand tons of fruits and vegetables were processed by Tunisia's canning industry.

Cattle and poultry are being raised on a large scale to produce more meat, milk, cheese, and eggs—all nutritious foods. Production has been increasing steadily; some of these products are already being exported to Europe. One agricultural expert said, "Tunisia might one day become the Argentina of the Mediterranean region." He meant that both Tunisia and Argentina produce many different kinds of farm products.

THE FORESTS AND THE SEAS

Forests cover about 8 percent of Tunisia and represent 14 percent of all productive lands. Although several types of trees are found, only one—the cork tree—can be used in industry. Cork tree forests are located in the northwest, and they produce an average of eighty-five thousand tons of cork every year, making Tunisia the eighth largest producer of cork in the world. Most of the harvest used to be exported just as it came from the tree or else in the form of bottle corks, but now there is a factory that processes cork for industrial use.

Another natural product found in Tunisia is alfa grass, which grows in the semiarid steppe and the desert. About one hundred thousand tons of it is harvested every year, most of which is used in the manufacture of paper. In 1963 a factory was built in Kasserine to process the alfa grass. This factory produces over one hundred tons of paper every day—enough to satisfy the country's needs—plus twenty-four thousand tons of paper paste, which is exported to Europe.

Peasants living near the sea used to rely both on fishing and farming for their livelihood. In the last ten years, however, fishing has become a major industry, with production varying between twenty and thirty thousand tons a year. Around Mahdia, Sousse, and Sfax, fishing is done at night. The fishermen use lamps to attract sardine, anchovy, and mackerel, and factories in Sousse and Mahdia can about twenty-two hundred tons of sardines each year. Tuna fishing, a spectacular and difficult activity, is practiced mostly in the north in June. The catch averages over eight hundred tons a year. About two hundred tons of tuna are canned in olive oil each year by factories in the north. Lobsters and oysters are also found west of Bizerte. Finally, about one hundred tons of sponges are gathered off the shores of Sfax and the island of Djerba.

INDUSTRY

Under the nationalization law signed by President Bourguiba in 1964, the government receives the profits of all of Tunisia's industry. It invests some of this money in industry, manufacturing, and mining.

Some of this money was spent for modernizing and expanding existing industries such as textiles and clothing, soapmaking from olive oil, and extracting perfumes and essential oils from the flowers of orange, jasmine, pine, and lemon. The surplus products from these industries are exported.

Most efforts, however, have been used to create new and larger industries. Since 1965, when a large oil field was discovered south of Gabès, the petroleum industry has grown rapidly. Since that time, many oil companies have been searching for oil throughout Tunisia and in the Mediterranean Sea off Tunisia's eastern coast. In 1971 total oil production reached five million tons and is expected to top nine million tons per year by 1976, bringing an additional income of about US $100 million to Tunisia each year.

A steel mill was built in the late 1960s in Menzel Bourguiba. This mill uses all of the iron ore mined in Tunisia and exports steel products to the rest of Africa. The chemical industry has also been growing quite rapidly, using Tunisia's large deposits of phosphates and natural gas. Shipyards have been opened in the ports of Bizerte and Sfax. Now they repair ships, but soon they will begin building them as well.

There are also some smaller industries that make products such as car batteries, spark plugs, fertilizers, aluminum kitchen utensils, and explosives. These are usually small, privately owned operations, not un-

Men load bags to be exported onto a Tunisian ship at a port.

78

Conveyor belts send baskets to the lower level of a fruit processing, canning, and packaging plant in Tunis, where they are packed with fruit.

der the nationalization law. They supply only the local market. A tire factory, partly owned by a large American tire manufacturer, makes all the tires the country needs. Many factories import the parts for different products and assemble them locally; among these are factories that make television sets and motor vehicles using parts from France. Tunisia also makes all the cement, bricks, tile, and other building materials that it needs.

POWER

Lack of money is not the only reason it has been difficult for Tunisia to expand its

80

industry. Lack of sufficient electricity presents another problem. There is not enough electricity in the country to run the manufacturing; electricity is made from such natural resources as petroleum, natural gas, coal, and water. Because Tunisia has few natural power sources, it must depend largely on imports. There are only one or two rivers that have water all year round; thus, hydraulic energy (water power) represents less than 2 percent of the country's power resources. Tunisia also lacks coal deposits. Tunisia had to import coal and oil at a great expense to supply the major cities with electricity.

Oil and natural gas deposits recently found near Gabès are now being used. These fields will also supply the entire south with electric power for homes and farms. Until recently, electricity was unavailable in this region.

Today most large cities and towns in Tunisia have electricity, but there are many villages without it. Since there is still not enough energy available and industry usually gets electricity before homes do, it will be some time before every Tunisian household has electricity. In the far distant future, perhaps the heat and light from the desert sun will be turned into energy and used to make electricity. This process, however, is very expensive and Tunisia cannot yet afford it.

BUSINESS

Since 1956 Tunisia's balance of trade has always shown consistent deficits, which means that Tunisia imports more goods than it exports. To maintain a good balance of trade, a country's imports should be worth about the same as its exports. Before 1962 Tunisia exported mostly farm products and a few minerals, and imported consumer goods such as cars, radios, and clothing. After 1962, however, the government slowed down the import of such consumer goods and began to buy more industrial equipment. Because raw materials were processed as much as possible, more jobs were created for Tunisians and their products were worth more in foreign markets. Whenever possible, consumer goods were manufactured locally instead of being imported.

As a result of these policies, trade in both directions increased and the trade deficit decreased. But Tunisia must continue to import expensive equipment for industry, transportation, and research.

France continues to be Tunisia's main trade partner. In the last few years, however, Tunisia has begun to trade more with other nations—especially with West Germany, Italy, and the United States. In 1956 France bought 50 percent of Tunisia's exports and supplied 60 percent of its imports; in 1971 the respective figures were 19 percent and 31 percent.

The Central Bank of Tunisia issues currency and controls the movement of money in and out of Tunisia. There is also a kind of stock market, said to be unique in North Africa, and other financial institutions such as mutual funds and savings and loan associations.

Enchantment of Tunisia

"Tunisia the green, you charmed my heart, with your beautiful gazelles, your white beaches, and your blue skies," says an old, popular folk song. For many years, Tunisia has been known as a unique melting pot for Eastern and Western cultures. One French writer commented that Tunisia has the colors, the blinding light, and the mystery of Africa, the delicate and artistic features of the Middle East, and the practicality and progress of the West.

THE WHITE CITY

A glimpse of Tunis from the air shows why this city is called "The White City."

Practically every building is painted white, and the whole city looks like a white cape that was casually thrown on a small piece of land squeezed between two small lakes. To the north and south, Tunis is bordered by hills. Hundreds of years ago, the waters of Lake Tunis, east of the city, reached much farther inland than they do today, to a point that is still called Bab-el-Bhar, or "the Gate of the Sea." Thus, Tunis has natural protection on all sides.

Beginning in the late nineteenth century, the land that used to be covered by water, near the city, was used by the Europeans to build what is today the modern section of Tunis. The modern sec-

Columns at the Mosque of Zitouna are lit at night. This mosque is one of the most famous examples of Islamic architecture in Tunisia.

tion literally surrounds the old section, known as the *medina*. Almost every city in North Africa has a medina.

The medina is by far the most picturesque part of Tunis. It has small, narrow streets that are not even wide enough for cars. It contains very old mosques and its many beautiful, old homes were once residences of rich Tunisians. Even the king used to live there. It is also in the medina that the city's old *aswak,* or markets, are found (the singular of aswak is *souk*). The aswak are usually covered streets that look like tunnels, with small holes left in the ceilings to let the sun in. Each souk specializes in one product, such as the souk for clothes, the souk for jewelry, and the souk for hats.

On the outer edges of the medina are many gates that used to be closed at night. Even some of the aswak had their own gates as well. Today the gates are not used and large avenues run all around the medina, forming a kind of loop.

Eastward from Bab-el-Bhar, modern Tunis has grown and expanded. The heart

Tunis, "The White City."

of this section of town is Bourguiba Avenue, about a mile long, with a center strip reserved for pedestrians. Bourguiba Avenue is lined with trees and there are outdoor stands where florists sell their flowers. This is where many of the city's department stores, banks, theaters, fashionable shops, and cafés are located. In the evening, when the workday is over, many people stroll up and down this avenue. Others sit in the sidewalk cafés talking with their friends or simply watching people coming and going.

As in many other cities in the world, traffic jams are very common in Tunis. A multitude of very small cars painted red and white cut in and out of traffic: these are cabs, quite appropriately called *taxi-bébé* (baby cabs) because of their size. These tiny vehicles will take a passenger from one end of the city to the other for pennies, but they are very hard to stop. Blue-painted buses also travel throughout the city, always seeming to carry twice as many people as they should.

Tunisia's tallest building, the twenty-five story Africa on Bourguiba Avenue, was completed in 1968. It is a hotel, though there are also offices, restaurants, a theater, and a drugstore in the building.

On the western edge of the medina there used to be an old fortress known as the *kasbah* (qasbah), which was used to guard one of the main gates to the city. Like the medinas, the kasbahs are common in North Africa. Tunis's kasbah has been demolished and the space has been used to build office buildings. Near what used to

be the kasbah are found many government buildings, including the president's office.

There are many small parks and gardens scattered around the city, but the largest and most beautiful one is Belvedere Park. Many Tunisians go there on weekends to picnic, visit the fine zoo, or just to walk. On top of a small hill in Belvedere Park is an observation point from which there is a breathtaking view of the whole city of Tunis. The park is located in one of the wealthiest sections of Tunis, and many foreign ambassadors, government officials, and Tunisian businessmen own homes there. Not too far away is a new American-owned hotel and the huge municipal stadium, where soccer games are played on Sundays.

Southwest of Belvedere Park is the suburb of Bardo. The world-famous museum in Bardo has a very rich collection of mosaics from the Roman era, as well as many other remains of the many civilizations that flourished in Tunisia. The museum building was once the palace of Tunisian kings.

About ten miles east of Tunis is Carthage. This city was founded in 814 B.C. by Queen Elissa of Phoenicia. It became a major power—the center of the Punic Empire, which stretched across all of North Africa. In three great wars Carthage was defeated by the Roman Empire. Destroyed at the end of the Third Punic War in 148 B.C., it was rebuilt in 44 B.C. Tunis became the capital of the Roman province called Africa, which included almost all of the former Punic Empire. Until 1235, Carthage remained a major city. Then nearby Tunis was made capital of what was then the Arab territory of Ifriqya.

Today Carthage is just a suburb of Tunis. Pleasant estates mingle with ancient temples and statues. The amphitheater built by the Romans, almost as large as the Colosseum in Rome, has been rebuilt and is used for music festivals during the summer.

The village of Sidi-Bou-Said is located a few miles east of Carthage on a high hill dominating the Bay of Tunis. According to legend, Sidi-Bou-Said was a saint who could cure any illness and who watched from the top of his hill for any enemy ships approaching Tunis. Legend also says that the village was used as a harbor by the pirates of the Mediterranean.

Many international celebrities—actors, writers, dukes, and princes—have homes in Sidi-Bou-Said, where they spend their vacations or even live permanently. Sidi-Bou-Said is also a meeting place for artists, poets, and intellectuals who gather in the famous Café des Nattes to sip mint tea and talk about the latest films, plays, and novels, or listen to Tunisian classical music, called *ma'luf.* This music is an outgrowth of an old form called the *nawba,* which is an instrumental composition with verses and refrains that are sung aloud. Once there were twenty-four different nawba, but now only eleven of them are known. Each nawba was played at a particular hour of the day. By the end of a nawba, the tempo is often twice as fast as it was in the beginning.

MAJOR COASTAL CITIES

Bizerte This town, with its small but well-protected natural harbor, was also founded by the ancient Phoenicians, who called it Hippo-Diarrhytus. It is the oldest city in Tunisia. Until 1963, it served as an important military base for the North Atlantic Treaty Organization (NATO) and for France, but today it is a quiet town of about sixty thousand people. Thanks to a huge convention hall built in 1965 and equipped with the most modern facilities, the town is becoming a national and international convention center.

Bizerte is located on the northern edge of a small lake that is connected to the sea by a man-made canal. Like so many other Tunisian cities, it has an old medina with aswak, mosques, and a kasbah. There is also a small harbor used by fishing boats in the center of town. All around this harbor, there are picturesque cafés and restaurants that serve excellent seafood. People often spend evenings eating while watching the fishermen unload their catches.

A few miles from Bizerte is a 750-foot-high hill that is a favorite tourist spot. This hill is the northernmost tip of Africa and it overlooks all of Bizerte. Its seaside location makes skin diving and sailing popular in Bizerte, and the nearby sand dunes are used for camping.

Sfax With a population of about one hundred thousand, Sfax is Tunisia's second largest city. In the last few years, the rapid growth it has experienced has made it a major business city in Tunisia.

Sfax and the surrounding region have long been quite prosperous, thanks to the fine farmland which produces olive oil, cereals, and fruits. Sfax also has an active fishing industry, with a fleet of a thousand small boats and a few large ships.

The people of Sfax are known for their thrift, hard work, and independence. They were practically the only people in Tunisia to have actively resisted foreign invasions, especially those of the Arabs in the eleventh century and the Turks and French in the nineteenth century.

In recent years, many new industries have been established in Sfax, including plants that process olive oil, phosphates,

Sfax, Tunisia's second largest city.

fish, and fruits. The city is also a major railroad center, and after Tunis, its harbor is the second busiest in the nation.

Sousse Sousse was built in the ninth century B.C. by the Phoenicians, who called it Hadrumete. The second oldest city in Tunisia, Sousse was a busy harbor long before Carthage was founded. Since then it has been invaded many times, most recently in 1943 by the Germans. This attack led to heavy bombings by the Allies that destroyed a large portion of the city.

Today Sousse is still an active port, exporting alfa grass, salt, and olive oil. With a population of about seventy-five thousand, it is the third largest city in Tunisia. As in so many other parts of Tunisia, however, the traditional businesses of the city are quickly giving way to a new activity—tourism. Each year a growing number of tourists come to Sousse to enjoy its beautiful beaches and its many historical sites, including the Ribat, a fortress-monastery built by the Arabs in the eighth century. Families lived in very small cells, and the men were bound by vows to defend their country and their religion against all enemies.

Another famous historical site is the Catacombs, which are underground cemeteries where early Christians persecuted by the Romans were buried. The Catacombs, discovered in 1888, contain 15,000 tombs in underground galleries.

Sousse also has a fine museum containing some very well-preserved mosaics from the Roman period, as well as remains from the Punic and Arabic civilizations.

ATTRACTIONS OF THE SOUTH

In Tunis and the northern half of Tunisia are some uniquely Arabic sights such as the souk and the medina. Otherwise, the area resembles the well-developed regions of many other countries.

Only 350 miles south of Tunis, however, is what appears to be a totally different world. Here the landscape seems endless and totally barren, with no apparent life whatsoever—almost like the surface of the moon! Temperatures may reach 115 degrees Fahrenheit during the day and dip to 40 degrees Fahrenheit at night. This is the great Sahara, the desert that separates North Africa from the rest of the continent.

The unsuspecting person may think he is the victim of a mirage when he suddenly sees a man or a camel moving on the horizon. More often than not, this would be the case—mirages (imaginary sights caused by light and heat waves) are very frequent in the desert. Sometimes, though, the vision may indeed be real, for there are a few people who live in this part of Tunisia.

These hardy people are mostly Berbers, and they have lived in the desert region for many centuries. During that time, the Berbers have developed some remarkable ways to adapt to their environment. In some villages the people live in large pits dug directly into the ground. In the walls of the pits, horizontal holes are dug, each large enough to be a room. Each room is used for a specific purpose, such as

A Berber woman and boy near their tent in the desert.

cooking, sleeping, or sheltering animals. Since these rooms are naturally insulated, they stay very cool during the day and warm at night. Inside the rooms are shelves, benches, and beds dug directly into the rock. Furniture is unnecessary. When more rooms are needed, they are just dug into the walls of the pit. This type of architecture is so practical and so well suited for the climate that it is used to build many hotels for tourists throughout the south.

The desert Berbers lead a very harsh life. They raise a few animals, mostly goats and sheep, and they grow a little barley, but they have very little water. The government is trying to dig wells in their villages or to bring water in by building canals that connect with neighboring areas.

Despite their physical isolation from the rest of the country, the Berbers remain an important part of Tunisia and of Tunisia's people. Their survival in the face of such difficulty makes them a symbol of Tunisia's efforts to develop itself into a modern nation with determination as the only major natural resource.

Handy Reference Section

INSTANT FACTS

Political:
Official Name—*Al Jumhuriya at Tunusiya* (The Republic of Tunisia)
Capital—Tunis
Official Language—Arabic
Literacy Rate—32%
Monetary Unit—dinar (1,000 milliemes = 1 dinar = about US $2)
Flag—Red, with a white circle in the middle; in this circle, a five-pointed star within a red crescent

Geographical:
Area—63,380 square miles
Greatest Length (north to south)—480 miles
Greatest Width (east to west)—200 miles
Highest Point—5,064 feet
Lowest Point—100 feet below sea level

HOLIDAYS AND SPECIAL EVENTS

Religious holidays follow the lunar calendar and change from year to year.
March 20—Independence Day
April—Orange Festival
April 9—Martyr's Day
May—Horse racing competition for the President's Cup; International Fair in Tunis (every four years)
May 1—Labor Day
June—Soccer championships
June 1—Victory Day
June 2—Youth Day
July—Coral Festival in Tabarka; Carthage Festival
July 25—Republic Day
August—Sidi-Bou-Said Festival
August 3—Habib Bourguiba's Birthday
August 13—Women's Day
October 15—Evacuation Day

POPULATION

Population—5,137,000 (1970 estimate)
Population Density—80 persons per square mile
Population Growth Rate—2.5 percent per year
Life Expectancy—51.7 years

Population of Principal Cities (1970 estimate):
Bardo	50,000
Bizerte	65,000
Gabès	45,000
Gafsa	45,000
Sfax	100,000
Sousse	75,000
Tunis	800,000

Population of Governorates (1966 census):
Beja	321,000
Bizerte	330,000
Gabès	204,000
Gafsa	321,000
Jendouba	255,000
Kairouan	278,000
Kasserine	212,000
Le Kef	311,000
Medenine	242,000
Nabeul	324,000
Sousse	521,000
Sfax	425,000
Tunis	790,000

YOU HAVE A DATE WITH HISTORY

12,000 B.C.—Maurusien people arrive
7000 B.C.—Capsien people arrive
814 B.C.—Quart Hadasht (Carthage) founded; Punic Empire established
535 B.C.—Carthage declares war on Greece
264-241 B.C.—First Punic War
219-201 B.C.—Second Punic War
149-146 B.C.—Third Punic War
148 B.C.—Destruction of Carthage; beginning of Roman occupation
44 B.C.—Carthage rebuilt by Romans
180 A.D.—Christianity brought to Africa
238—Africa's independence from Rome declared
439—Vandals occupy Carthage
534-647—Byzantine rule
647—Islam brought to Africa by Arabs
670—Kairouan founded
670-973—Arab rule
695—Carthage falls to Arabs
916—Mahdia founded
973—Fatimids conquer Egypt; Cairo founded
1050—Bologuin descendants switch allegiance from Egypt to Baghdad
1051—Nomadic groups invade Kairouan
1087—Roman Catholic pope attacks Tunis
1148—Normans capture Mahdia
1160—Almohades capture Ifriqya
1230—Hafsite dynasty founded
1236—Tunis becomes capital of Tunisia
1270—Crusaders led by Louis IX of France attack Tunis; Louis IX dies in Carthage

1432—Alphonse V of Aragon attacks Tunis
1534—Turks attack Tunisia
1535—Carlos V of Spain retakes Tunis
1540—Carlos V retakes Monastir; Spanish protectorate established over Tunis
1574—Turks retake Tunis and occupy Tunisia; Ottoman Empire begins
1631—Murad Bey becomes pasha
1702—Ibrahim Sharif overthrows Murad dynasty and becomes pasha, bey, and dey
1710—Hussainite dynasty begins
1878—Congress of Berlin
1881—Tunisia becomes a French protectorate
1903—Birth of Habib Bourguiba, August 3
1920—First political party, Destour Party, organized
1934—Néo-Destour Party organized by Bourguiba
1946—General Union of Tunisian Workers (UGTT) organized
1956—Independence, March 20; first elections, March 25; Assembly holds first meeting, April 8
1957—Monarchy replaced by a republic headed by Bourguiba
1958—French air force attacks Sakiet-Sidi-Youssef
1959—University of Tunis founded; constitution becomes effective, June 1
1961—Battle with France over Bizerte
1964—Foreign-owned land nationalized, May 12
1965—Television begins in Tunisia; oil and natural gas discovered at El Borma
1969—Major floods, September 25-29
1973—New Tunis airport opens

Index